From Image to Likeness

I Become What I Am

Archpriest Vladimir Berzonsky

St. Tikhon's Seminary Press

©2003 Vladimir Berzonsky

ISBN 1-878997-74-2

St. Tikhon's Seminary Press
P.O. Box B
South Canaan PA 18459

bookstore@stots.edu

Printed in the United States of America

From Image to Likeness

First Day
CHOOSING THE TWELVE
Mark 3:13:19

And He went up on the mountain and called to Him those He Himself wanted. And they came to Him. Then He appointed twelve, that they might be with Him and that He might send them out to preach, and to have power to heal sicknesses and to cast out demons. Simon, to whom He gave the name Peter; James son of Zebedee and John the brother of James, to whom He gave the name Boanerges, that is 'Sons of Thunder,' Andrew, Philip, Bartholomew, Matthew, Thomas, James the son of Alphaeus, Thaddeus, Simon the Canaanite, and Judas Iscariot, who also betrayed Him. And they went into a house.

This is an exciting moment in the life of Jesus Christ. He knows what He wants to say to the world but how will He say it? He understood that He would not be able to do it alone. First, He realized very well that His life would be the price to pay for telling the people of the world how wrong they are, and what they must do in order to correct their lives and to transform the world itself. Even we who are baptized in His name and bear not just His name as Christians, but who say that we are ready to carry our own crosses just as He did — we are not easily corrected.

Another great problem is the method of getting His message to humanity. There were no newspapers, magazines, certainly none of the devices like the space satellites we have today that can send signals everywhere on earth in a few seconds. Remember, first came the Church, then the Bible. There were no writings yet, about His life, teachings, death and resurrection. He formed a company of disciples who became the Church.

He chose twelve men whom He considered capable of carrying His gospel to the ends of the earth. It would take love of Him; belief that what He said had come about. It would take courage, because they would end as He did — and they knew it. They were not at all of the same personality types and temperaments; indeed, they might be seen as contrasts in natures. After Pentecost we find in Acts that the initial leaders were Peter and John — at least we find them often together. Peter, the consummate person in action, was a take-charge sort, bold and impulsive, eager to jump into things. John, on the other hand a younger man, loving meditation and solitude, a deep thinker who looks before he acts, as we saw when the two of them ran to the tomb, John there first, yet reluctant to enter, while the older, slower Peter just kept barging through the darkness.

Notice the difference between Thomas, a skeptic, not trusting to the eyewitness accounts of others, and Bartholomew, somebody who eagerly believed and trusted what he heard and saw. Remember that Matthew was a tax collector and collaborator with the Roman authorities over and against his own people, while Simon was a rebel, one of the Zealots who were part of any move that opposed Roman rule, a man who despised those who paid taxes and looked down on those who collaborated with the occupiers of the land. Gazing at them on an icon it's hard to distinguish one from another; however, they were individuals, with personalities of their own. Yet they surrendered their wills to the will of the Father in heaven. All were men of courage, of devotion to Christ, eager to give their souls and bodies to Him. What of us? We call ourselves Christians and say we belong to His Church. Do we have the same love, faith, valor, and willingness to give our lives for His sake? How many of our talents do we place at the service of the Lord we love?

Second Day
SATAN THE DIVIDER
Mark 3:20-27

Then the multitude came together again, so that they could not so much as eat bread. But when His own people heard about this, they went out to lay hold of Him, for they said, 'He is out of His mind.' And the scribes who came down from Jerusalem said 'He has Beelzebub' and, 'By the ruler of the demons He casts out demons.' So He called them to Himself and said to them in parables, 'How can Satan cast out Satan? If a kingdom is divided against itself, that kingdom cannot stand. And if a house is divided against itself, that house cannot stand. And if Satan has risen up against himself, and is divided, he cannot stand, but has an end. No one can enter a strong man's house and plunder his goods, unless he first binds the strong man. And then he will plunder his house.'

The Jews believed that Jesus was a sorcerer. They refused to accept His own witness that all of His power came from God the Father through the Holy Spirit. No matter what He said or did, even to raising up several persons from death, they continued to attribute His great miracles to evil spirits or to mere trickery. Using their logic against them, He said that if their argument were true, it would make Satan his own worst enemy, because then he would be working against himself.

He goes on to add a deep mystery: The world is like a house occupied by a powerful person. He is safe within it, including all who live with him. What would happen, however, if there came a man even stronger than he? And that man would enter the house, overwhelm the powerful tenant, and then tie him up securely. Whatever he wants to do after that he is free to do. He can subsequently take his time going from room to room finding and stealing all the valuables and removing them.

The meaning is quite clear: Jesus is telling His audience that He Himself is that strong visitor — let's call Him a thief! The house is the world, and the tenant is Satan. In another place He said that His battle is not with humans, but with the evil spirits of darkness. It was inevitable that the devil would realize the power and source of His authority and do his best to rid the world of Christ.

Have you ever been misunderstood? When you had made some gesture of friendship that was taken the wrong way, or said something intended to be kind and helpful, only to be criticized for it? Here is what happened to Jesus. Great crowds rushed to see His healing powers. They watched as He drove out demons; and yet the response from some was that He Himself was insane. Why is it that to live with anger, hostility, and crimes of passion, brutality and mass destruction is considered normal, then and now? After awhile we wrap ourselves with a protection of invulnerability by pretending evil things don't happen, or else we can take no notice of them and go on with our lives. The peace of Christ is ignored, misunderstood, or simply not wanted. How did we become like this?

To be His disciples we must point out the evil of it all. To restore the world to its original plan in God's eyes is to recognize the demonic for what it is, to reject as normal whatever is hateful, demeaning, sinful, lustful and corrupt. And we must begin with ourselves. To be His apostles is not for spectators, but for the actively engaged.

Third Day
THE UNPARDONABLE SIN
Mark 3:28-30

Truly I say to you, all sins will be forgiven the sons of men, and whatever blasphemies they may utter; but he who blasphemes against the Holy Spirit never has forgiveness, but is subject to eternal condemnation' — because they said 'he has an unclean spirit.'

The Son of God and the Holy Spirit are the two agents, or arms, of the heavenly Father. They are involved directly in the very creation of the universe. *The earth was a formless void and darkness covered the face of the deep, while* **a wind from God** *swept over the face of the waters* (Gen. 1:2). The Son is the Word of God, so that when the Father speaks, *Let there be light,* the very Word He utters (*Logos* in Greek) is the Son. And so it is with the elements of creation on each of the six days. *When God saw that it was good* it is God as Trinity that is meant, just as it is written: *Let us make man in our image, according to our likeness* (Gen. 1: 26) meaning clearly that the human being is made in the image of the three Persons of the Trinity.

When out of ignorance and mean-spiritedness the religious leaders of Jesus' day could no longer deny the evidence of their eyes that He was healing and performing miracles, they called Him a sorcerer who had received His powers from Satan. *He has an unclean spirit.* In their blindness to the God they claimed to pray to, they were saying that God works through the devil. No greater perversion of truth can be imagined. They no longer searched for truth; they rejected it when it stood before them. They were no different from Pontius Pilate, a pagan without any visible faith in a deity. Worse, because Pilate might claim never to have been exposed to the God of Abraham, Isaac and Jacob. Unfortunately, he's quite the modern man.

It appears at first as though the Holy Spirit were unforgiving. But it's the blasphemer who feels he has no need of forgiveness, just as he feels he is himself the source of truth. In fact, the Orthodox Christians begin every gathering, certainly each divine liturgy, with a prayer to "the Holy Spirit, the Comforter, and Spirit of truth." The Spirit comforts us with truth; for without truth we are more than restless, we are hopelessly lost. And no one is more lost than the one who not only has no direction, but also denies there is a purpose to life. The blasphemer against the Spirit is never forgiven, because in order to be forgiven one must accept forgiveness. To do so requires that he recognizes he has a need to be forgiven. If in your mind you believe you have done nothing wrong or sinful, the very thought of remorse, penance and pardon is repulsive to you.

Here is a frightful condemnation — eternal expulsion from the presence of God. Jesus is saying this to the Pharisees and Sadducees who opposed Him. He Himself is willing to forgive all who sin against Him; but the sin against the Holy Spirit has eternal consequences. They are refusing to recognize the power of the Spirit that is ushering God's Kingdom into time and history. Maybe you know somebody like that — pray you are not one of them. They distort good intentions into something perverse. Gogol said, "How sad are they who do not see the goodness in the good." They sniff around like dogs, searching for something or somebody to criticize and mock.

Ask yourself: Am I searching for signs of God's grace operating in the world, or do I explain everything away? Do I see the goodness, kindness, gentleness, good intentions, and blessedness in people, or do I find only fault with them all?

Fourth Day
EARS TO HEAR
Mark 4:1-9

And behold, a sower went out to sow, and it happened as he sowed, that some seed fell by the wayside, and the birds of the air came and devoured it. Some fell on stony ground, where it did not have much earth; and immediately it sprang up because it had no depth of earth. But when the sun was up it was scorched, and because it had no root it withered away. And some seed fell among thorns, and the thorns grew up and choked it, and it yielded no crop. But other seed fell on good ground and yielded a crop that sprang up, increased and produced some thirtyfold, some sixty, some a hundred.' And He said to them, 'He who has ears to hear, let him hear.'

By people who have hearing ears Jesus of course doesn't mean those who are hard of hearing, but those who take in more than sounds — people who comprehend the hidden meanings of His teachings and apply the messages to themselves. Eliza Doolittle in *My Fair Lady* screamed: "Word, words, words! I'm so sick of words!" Indeed, so are we. We cannot escape them. Not in restaurants, nor elevators, nor on buses — everywhere are sounds, and they're so difficult to filter out. Like so many seeds of Christ's parable, they don't bear fruit. But if we attune our hearing to His Word, we find ourselves listening intently, fearful of missing a single phrase. Let His voice carried in the Holy Gospel captivate your inner ear, whispering the way of truth and life, calling you from among the way of lost souls and onto the narrow path that the saints in every generation have trod, through this world and beyond death, into the Kingdom that awaits us. Learn to shut off the static of gossip, of angry shouts, of the voices from your memory bank that whisper about past offenses, intimidations, times of weakness that you have confessed and put behind you, and you will be ready to hear the still, tiny voice once heard by the prophet Elijah. Actually I've always looked forward each year to preaching on this text. I feel that Jesus had the clergy in mind when He offered this parable, because it is such a comfort to us.

How can it be, I wonder, that so many seem not to be affected by the beauty of the liturgy, the eloquence and mystery of the hymns and prayers, the examples of the good people of God with whom they pray, and yes, the inspirational messages they hear week after week, not necessarily from the homilies, but from the very words of the sacred and inspired Bible itself? Then I consider what may be preventing the meaning from getting through. Some simply have never been exposed to the depths of the faith in their homes or family upbringing. More and more it's the way of American life. The television has replaced reading the Bible and other worthwhile literature. Some others never listen, because they never stop talking. The culture we live in is made up of opinion makers and those who feel that they need no education, starting every comment with "That's what I think." There is no basic truths or eternal wisdom to them, only a matter of random opinions. Still others have a short attention span. They come to the liturgy, open their souls to the Lord, truly feel uplifted by the Holy Spirit, but the aura of sanctity lasts halfway across the parking lot.

Then, of course, we have the blessed ones Jesus spoke of whose hearts are like the good earth. They absorb the water of the Spirit, the fertilizer of Christ's words, the sunshine of the Father's benediction, and they never get enough of it all. Praise the Lord! May their kind continue to increase! They make it all worthwhile — for Him and for us.

Fifth Day
FOR GOD AND COUNTRY
Matthew 22:16:21

Then the Pharisees went and plotted how they might entangle Him in His talk. And they sent to Him their disciples with the Herodians, saying, 'Teacher, we know that you are true, and teach the way of God in truth; nor do You care about anyone, for You do not regard the person of men. Tell us, therefore, what do You think? Is it lawful to pay taxes to Caesar or not?' But Jesus perceived their wickedness and said, 'Why do you test Me, you hypocrites? Show me the tax money.' So they brought Him a denarius. And He said to them, 'Whose image and inscription is this?' They said to Him, 'Caesar's.' And He said to them, 'Render therefore to Caesar the things that are Caesar's, and to God the things that are God's.'

Paying taxes was a mighty issue in Christ's time. Jews thought of the land as owned by the Lord, but occupied and usurped by the Romans. If Jesus were for payment of taxes He would be considered a traitor to His people. If He said no, He would be treated as a revolutionary and be subject to arrest. He lifted the problem above the case at hand. Our Lord Jesus Christ is not describing a conflict between commitments. We have our duties and loyalties both to the Lord Almighty, and to the nation we live in. We pledge our allegiance to both powers that transcend our personal selves: to the nation, but first to the One Who is above all nations and persons. Our coins are stamped with the profiles of past presidents; however we are stamped with the image of God. It means that we must return to Him what is His within us. We live in a wonderful nation and we pay our taxes willingly, just as we pay our debts to this society at times, even at the risk of our lives during war times. We Orthodox Christians are not like those sects who enjoy the privilege of American citizenship, yet refuse to pay the price of patriotism.

On the other hand, we uphold our greater loyalty first to the Living God, the Holy Trinity, above and beyond every earthly allegiance. We understand that we are marked with God's image. We are like the lost coin of Luke 15:8 that Jesus Christ came from Heaven to find. His greatest wish is to return us to His Father.

There's more to the analogy of coin to soul. Coins are defaced in time. They lose the image of Caesar. The faces of our American presidents eventually wear off. Despite their hardness, in time they are worn out and reclaimed, either replaced with another imprint or lost. That cannot happen to the image of God embossed on your soul. No matter how you may deface your body with gluttony, alcoholism, drugs, or loose living, you will not lose the Image of God. It doesn't mean that you can redeem it for a place in heaven after this lifetime is over. Quite the contrary. Because God entrusted you with His image, He expects you to cherish it, increase it, and invest it in a worthwhile way of living. Put another way, while you are alive, you have the potential to become like God. It's not too much to say so. St. Athanasius the Great told us: "God became man [*or* human] so that man [each human being] can become God through grace." Through prayer, fasting, care for others, charity and acts of good will you are encouraged to live as God's ambassador. As an Orthodox Christian you are commanded to do so. But you have the freedom to do as you wish — grow in grace to a likeness of the Lord, or waste the gift of God in ways that shame you and cause suffering to Him who made you.

Sixth Day
THE EARTH AS A VINEYARD
Matthew 21:33-42

Hear another parable: There was a certain landowner who planted a vineyard and set a hedge around it, dug a winepress in it and built a tower. And he leased it to vinedressers and went into afar country. Now when vintage time drew near, he sent his servants to the vinedressers, that they might receive its fruit. And the vinedressers took his servants, beat one, killed one, and stoned another. Again he sent other servants, more than the first, and they did likewise to them. Then last of all he sent his son to them, saying, 'They will respect my son.' But when the vinedressers saw the son, they said among themselves, 'This is the heir. Come, let us kill him and seize his inheritance.' So they took him and cast him out of the vineyard and killed him. Therefore, when the owner of the vineyard comes, what will he do to those vinedressers?' They said to Him, 'He will destroy those wicked men miserably, and lease his vineyard to other vinedressers who will render to him the fruits in their seasons.' Jesus said to them, 'Have you never read in the Scriptures, **The stone which the builders rejected has become the chief cornerstone. This was the Lord's doing, and it is marvelous in our eyes?'**

Jesus is really addressing His fellow Hebrews. They understood Him well. They realized that they were chosen by God to take ownership of the world, to set an example for all other tribes and nations, teaching them what is God's will on earth. And they failed Him miserably. God is the **landowner,** the Hebrews are the **vinedressers,** the prophets are the **servants,** and Christ Jesus the **son and heir.** He is predicting His death, and the judgment that will follow. He also predicted the gift of spiritual legacy to the Gentiles:

Therefore I say to you, the kingdom of God will be taken from you and given to a nation bearing the fruit of it (21:43).

But how are we *bearing the fruit of it?* How are we treating God's precious earth? No serious person, certainly no scientist can look at the universe and consider it to be randomly organized and accidental in structure. The world that produces a variety of life forms didn't just happen. It was planned, planted and claimed by God. We humans too often treat it as though it were ours to do with as we please — to pollute, ravage, disrupt, destroy as we see fit — and our nations do likewise. We feel it appropriate to destroy and defile, ignoring the consequences for the future. But the Lord has already claimed it in Jesus Christ His Son. He will demand a response from us. Those who ignore or defy Him will have to give an answer. This is the ecological meaning of the parable. It's a wonderful tribute to their faith that so many true believers will march and speak out in protest against abortions and the logical next stage of death affirmations, euthanasia, but why do we not have such a vision of life that embraces the animals and vegetations? To protect animals and plants from extinction is a Christian responsibility.

The theologically important point is that Jesus Christ Himself is the chief cornerstone, or keystone, of the entire Church. There is no vicar who takes His place. There are not millions of individual cornerstones of their own making, nor are there multiple fragments of the True Church. The Church is one, joined in time and space. Wherever a valid Eucharist is celebrated, Christ Himself is both Celebrant and Sacrifice. The builders are the Hebrew nation. As they have rejected Jesus as the true Christ, it is the Gentiles who have been incorporated into the structure. They have replaced the Hebrew nation as builders.

Seventh Day
WHY DON'T ALL LISTENERS GET THE MESSAGE?
Luke 8:11-15

Now the parable is this: The seed is the word of God. Those by the wayside are the ones who hear, then the devil comes and takes away the word out of their hearts, lest they should believe and be saved. But the ones on the rock are those who, when they hear, receive the word with joy, and these have no root, who believe for a while and in time of temptation fall away. Now the ones that fell among thorns are those who, when they have heard, go out and are choked with cares, riches, and pleasures of life, and bring no fruit to maturity. But the ones that fell on the good ground are those who, having heard the word with a noble and good heart, keep it and bear fruit with patience.'

This is the only parable that Jesus explains — not to the crowd, but to His disciples. Interesting, that they should not totally understand its meaning. Also, it demonstrates that Jesus felt it has a special significance.

There are four kinds of earth in Palestine, not a region noted for its lush and fertile soil:

1. Farmers set the earth in long, narrow strips, much like the furrows in our fields. The planters and tillers would walk between the furrows, so that the pathway which had been trodden over the years became too hard to receive the seed.

2. Some earth was little more than a shallow covering over nearly solid rock beneath it. One would hardly expect roots to grow very deep.

3. It's difficult to clear the land sufficiently to remove all the seeds producing thorns, just as with us dandelions and flat leaves spring up along with the good growth.

4. The ground being so hardscrabble in Palestine, high quality, deep, rich soil is a priceless treasure cherished by any farmer.

The trodden path stands for the types who say they've seen it all. Nothing can reach them, not dynamic homilies, not gentle persuasion, and not sincere, heartfelt words from a pleading soul. They shut themselves off to all forms of urging. Indeed, they make a game of "Try and influence me." Deep within themselves they are pathetic, lonely people; yet they refuse to descend into the depths of their souls where it pains. The surface folks are called shallow for good cause. They never do spend much time reasoning out their values and objectives. They read opinion polls. Talk show hosts, media stars, athletes, and other such "celebrities" manipulate their minds. They don't have convictions; they have opinions. And their opinions change by the day and hour. The weeds and thorns grow up along with the prayers and church attendance. It's something they indulge in, along with all the other events and routine happenings that crowd in and leave such people exhausted at the end of the day with little to show for their weariness but a general malaise that they try to dispel by sitting in front of the television and flipping through the channels searching for something they will never find, because they don't know what they're looking for and wouldn't recognize it if they were to come upon it.

The Lord Jesus is saying: Be satisfied with one out of five. Who knows? The Holy Spirit is alive and well and working in the hearts of all the above. It may be that some of them may have an attitude transplant. He or she may just evaluate his life style and turn his life around. Miracles are what we do best.

Eighth Day
THE LAMP UNDER A BASKET
Mark 4:21-25

Also He said to them, 'Is a lamp brought to be put under a basket or under a bed? Is it not to be set on a lampstand? For there is nothing hidden which will not be revealed, nor has anything been kept secret but that it should come to light. If anyone has ears to hear, let him hear.' Then He said to them, 'Take heed what you hear. With the same measure you use, it will be measured to you; and to you who hear, more will be given. For whoever has, to him will more be given; but whoever does not have, even what he has will be taken from him.'

Truth not only should not be out of sight, it must not be hidden. That's like putting a bowl over a lamp. Several pastor friends of mine left their parishes. I asked them why, and they said they felt put upon by a few who caused them grief. "But surely there are kind, good, positive thinking people," I said. "Yes, but they never speak out," was the reply. The history of the Orthodox Church is replete with martyrs who spoke out and proclaimed Christ in the face of His enemies. The word *martyr* means witness to Christ.

For each of us a time comes to stand up for our faith: In the office when slander is spoken or off-color jokes repeated; in the classroom when students cheat or mock the weak; in the restaurant when it comes time to pray before eating. How ironic that Orthodox Christians were punished and put to death by Romans, Tartars, Muslims, and Communists for daring to display their faith in Christ openly and proudly, where here in America with our freedom to worship guaranteed by law, many of our people would rather conceal their faith and pass through society incognito.

We will be called to account for our witness to Christ's truth — if not in this world, then surely when we appear alone before the Throne of God in the assembly of the angels and saints of all the ages.

For whoever has, to him more will be given; but whoever does not have, even what he has will be taken from him.

It seems so unfair — downright undemocratic! To take away what one doesn't have? How can that be? Death ends life, and it ends all potential. Jesus says something similar in the parable of the talents (Matt. 25:29, Luke 19:26) where a nobleman sets off to a faraway land, distributing his wealth, or talents, to his servants as he felt their abilities to increase them warranted, demanding an accounting upon his return, expecting them to be doubled. It's not money but spiritual abilities that God requires from us. Those who have gifts they owe to their Creator, such as the aptitude to help others, to fill their souls with the peace of God that surpasses all understanding by opening their souls to Him, to develop the soul, that interior treasure called in Greek *nous*, and discover the Kingdom of heaven within us — all that will be taken away with the termination of life as we know it. That is, if we do nothing with them while we have the opportunity to do so.

To those who are making their way to the Kingdom even here in this lifetime, more will be given to them upon the completion of this phase of life. He and she who develop an appreciation of the sacred gifts will be fulfilled. What a blessed promise coming from our Lord Jesus! More peace, more love, more joy, more fellowship with the saints and angels, more awareness of the majesty and mystery of the Holy Trinity, more knowledge of the awesome wisdom of the Lord. What a glorious life awaits us on the other side!

Ninth Day
TWO VIRTUES IN A SINGLE SOUL
Luke 10:38-42

Now it happened as they went that He entered a certain village; and a certain woman named Martha welcomed Him into her house. And she had a sister called Mary, who also sat at Jesus' feet and heard His word. But Martha was distracted with much serving, and she approached Him and said, 'Lord, do You not care that my sister has left me to serve alone? Therefore tell her to help me.' And Jesus answered and said to her, 'Martha, Martha, you are worried and troubled about many things. But one thing is needed, and Mary has chosen that good part, which will not be taken away from her.'

How wonderful to know people like St. Luke, who observe what many others miss. In his gospel are numerous such precious vignettes. He has painted for us a portrait in words of people who surrounded our Lord, and the way His presence affected them.

Here is a family of three adults without parents or little children, the home of Lazarus and his two sisters, Martha and Mary. They lived not far from Jerusalem. Jesus would stay with them when He visited the city. On one such occasion, Mary became so intrigued with His words that she paused in her household duties to stay and imbibe His teachings. And it upset Martha. She tried to enlist Christ's aid to get her kid sister to help her.

Jesus, as He did frequently, used the occasion to teach a lesson to Martha. He repeats her name twice, and we can feel the tender sigh He gave: *You are worried and troubled by many things, but one thing is needed.* The one thing is the presence of God within our hearts. Many know about God: many less know

God. It's possible to spend a lifetime praying and attending church services, yet never feeling Him alive within the soul. True faith is complete acceptance of God's will for our lives. Without that we are always *worried and troubled by many things.*

Martha had broken the bond of unity between Christ and Mary without being aware of it. Jesus was to her at that instant a guest who needed to be served. She didn't understand that He was bringing to her home a treasure so rare that few in all history would have the opportunity to know it — He was offering Himself as a bond with His Father, and Mary was beginning to take advantage of the offer. Martha was missing the moment.

Carl Jung, the psychoanalyst, described most people as either extroverts like Martha, or introverts like Mary. Martha was practical and outgoing, like many activist Christians who raise funds, help the poor and needy, or who pitch themselves into worthwhile charitable causes. Mary types become monastics, go on retreats, pore over the holy scriptures, and seek places to be alone with the Lord. God loves each of us as we are, or better stated, as He would have us be. The Holy Theotokos and ever-virgin Mary was a composite of both types: Eager to work for the Lord, yet ready to listen for His word; knowing when to speak and when to listen, when to lead and when to follow, when to act and when to wait patiently for a signal, or simply refrain from acting.

The Holy Church is ever prepared to utilize the talents of all the Marthas and Marys of both sexes for the glory of God, happy to receive the gifts we each offer to the Lord and raise them up to Him, since they are ultimately not our possessions, but blessings of grace entrusted to our care. That's the meaning of the liturgical phrase: "Thine own of Thine own we offer Thee, on behalf of all, and for all."

Tenth Day
AT PEACE IN A STORM
Mark 4:35-41

Now when they had left the multitude, they took Him along in the boat as He was. And other little boats were also with Him. And a great windstorm arose, and the waves beat into the boat, so that it was already filling. But He was in the stern, asleep on a pillow. And they awoke Him and said to him, 'Teacher, do You not care that we are perishing?' Then He arose and rebuked the wind, and said to the sea, 'Peace, be still!' And the wind ceased and there was a great calm. But He said to them, 'Why are you so fearful? How is it that you have no faith?' And they feared exceedingly and said to one another, 'Who can this be, that even the wind and the sea obey Him!'

We can make an allegory of this unforgettable event in the memories of the apostles. We can say that the sea is life as we experience it with its many unforeseen stormy events that assail us, the little boat is our hearts and as long as we have Christ within us, there is nothing to fear. The Agent of the Father along with the Holy Spirit in creation obviously is in control of everything. We need only have faith in Him to experience His peace that transcends our understanding.

In our scientific era it's more difficult to imagine and indeed "believe in" this miracle than those that he performed in healing human beings. Yet we have the record of our native American Orthodox Christians who relate a similar miracle by St. Herman of Alaska. Once a tremendous, fearful hurricane was approaching. They call it *sunami*. They describe it with awe, knowing how destructive it can be. The elder, their beloved *apa* went to the shore and placed on the beach an icon of the Holy

Theotokos. Then he said, "The sunami will come this far, but no farther." And it happened as he had predicted. At this place in Mark's gospel is the first of three miracles that demonstrate the authority Christ has over the forces of evil and the demons of destruction and darkness. The other two follow, as one reads Mark through chapter 5. In them Jesus will prove His power over demonic possession and even death, the "last enemy."

Here in this episode we can understand the sheer terror of the apostles, those who unlike Jesus had spent their whole lives fishing on this very sea. Life is like that. We take for granted that our plans can be upset and torn apart at any moment by an incident that befalls either ourselves or somebody precious in our lives. Grin and bear it, we're advised — but we cannot smile and pretend we're pleased, although we do bear it, since there's no recourse. The apostles are right to fear the raging storm. Their lives are threatened by its diabolical waves. *Teacher, don't you care that we are perishing?* How many of us ever since down through the centuries have made our prayer to Him with a similar plea of desperation. *Don't you care?* How should He respond? To somehow convince us that indeed He does care? How would He do that, since we give no evidence of our trust in Him? We, like the apostles, have such a firm allegiance to the world invaded and claimed by Satan that we take for granted He understands and agrees with the condition of the fallen world.

That's the point. He doesn't agree. Just as He will dissuade the Gerasene demoniac from the tombs from his wish to be left to die in his agony, showing him that He has life to offer and a means of liberating him from demonic possession, so here He is at peace in turmoil. He expected those whom He chose to comprehend it. But it was too early for that.

Eleventh Day
THE MAN POSSESSED BY MANY DEMONS
Mark 5:1-20

Then they came to the other side of the sea, to the country of the Gadar- enes. And when He had come out of the boat, immediately there met him out of the tombs a man with an unclean spirit, who had his dwelling among the tombs; and no one could bind him, not even with chains, because he had often been bound with shackles and chains. And the chains had been pulled apart by him and the shackles broken in pieces; neither could anyone tame him. And always, night and day, he was in the mountains and in the tombs, crying out and cutting himself with stones. When he saw Jesus from afar, he ran and worshiped him. And he cried out with a loud voice and said, 'What have I to do with You, Jesus, Son of the most High God? I implore You by God that You do not torment me.' For He said to him, 'Come out of the man, unclean Spirit!' Then He asked him, 'What is your name?' And he answered, saying, 'My name is Legion; for we are many.' Also he begged Him earnestly that he would not send them out of the country. Now a large herd of swine was feeding there near the mountains. So all the demons begged Him, saying, 'Send us to the swine, that we may enter them.' And at once Jesus gave them permission. Then the unclean spirits went out and entered the swine (there were about two thousand); and the herd ran violently down the steep place into the sea, and drowned in the sea. So those who fed the swine fled, and they told it in the city and in the country. And they went out to see what it was that had happened. Then they came to Jesus, and saw the one who had been demon-possessed and had the legion, sitting and clothed and in his right mind. And they were afraid. And those who saw it told them how it happened to him who had been demon-possessed, and about the swine. Then they began to plead with Him to depart from that region.

Imagine yourself with Jesus in the boat that came ashore on the far side of the Sea of Galilee. It's twilight. Night approaches. Nearby swine herders are tending their pigs. From a cemetery a wild man emerges, ranting and flailing his arms about, nearly naked. He babbles and screams, speaking at times for himself, at other times as though he were a large body of people. To drive out the demons from such a sick person was not simple, not even for the Lord. He starts by ordering the demons out. Still, they remain. He then demands that the demon possessing the man reveal his name. The answer: I'm not alone in here. There are thousands of us, indeed as many as 6,000, the number of soldiers that comprised a Roman legion. What can He do to set the poor soul free from so many foul spirits? What to do with the demons? They cannot be exterminated.

God never destroys whatever He creates, no matter how far they may stray from His original intent when they were made — not humans, not angels, not even the demons. So He orders them to occupy the nearby swine rather than the demoniac, and to set him free from their occupancy. Does it mean that the Lord has no affection for pigs? Not at all. It shows us how precious each human soul is to the loving Lord. That man, that sad creature who had until then spent his life apart from all relatives and former friends, was dear to Jesus. And when the local residents learned what had happened, rather than praise the Lord for the miracle, they pleaded with Him to go away, back where He had come from. They must have loved their pigs more than the Lord of love and life.

Twelfth Day
FAITH BEYOND DEATH
Mark 5 :22-24, 35-43

And behold, one of the rulers of the synagogue came, Jairus by name. And when he saw Him, he fell at His feet and begged Him earnestly, saying, 'My little daughter lies at the point of death. Come and lay Your hands on her, that she may be healed, and she will live.' So Jesus went with him, and a great multitude followed Him and thronged Him . . . While he was still speaking, some came from the ruler of the synagogue's house who said, 'Your daughter is dead. Why trouble the Teacher any further?' As soon as Jesus heard the word that was spoken, He said to the ruler of the synagogue, 'Do not be afraid, only believe.' And He permitted no one to follow him except Peter, James, and John the brother of James. Then He came to the house of the ruler of the synagogue, and saw a tumult and those who wept and wailed loudly. When He came in, He said to them, 'Why make this commotion and weep? The child is not dead, but sleeping.' And they ridiculed Him. But when He had put them all outside, He took the father and the mother of the child, and those who were with Him, and entered where the child was lying. Then He took the child by the hand, and said to her, 'Talitha, cumi,' which is translated, 'Little girl, I say to you, arise.' Immediately the girl arose and walked, for she was twelve years of age. And they were overcome with great amazement. But He commanded them strictly that no one should know it, and said that something should be given to her to eat.

No grief is as great as the death of one's child. Death itself is unnatural. It comes about because of mankind's sin; however, one expects children to bury their aged parents, not the reverse. Jesus received so much humiliation and rejection from the religious leaders of His people. Now this ruler of the synagogue has a complete change of heart. He *fell at His feet and begged Him earnestly.* He set aside his dignity. It's not the time to pull rank and act the role of Mr. Big. Love does this to a person — not love of Jesus, but of one's own flesh and blood. He doesn't consider his status. Like the father of the Prodigal Son who ran down the road to greet his lost child, this man is reduced to a humility he may never have realized was in him. Nor is he concerned that this carpenter's son from Nazareth, whom he may have scorned and ridiculed earlier, but now calls "Lord," may be out of favor with all the religious potentates of the nation. All he cares about is that Jesus is a renowned healer, and possibly even One who can bring life back into the dead. How long did his gratitude last? Did this synagogue leader follow Christ, preach His gospel in the synagogue until he was himself removed? Or did he soon revert to being one of the mockers? And what of girl? Did she spend her life in appreciation of what God had done? I've known of those who pleaded with the Lord for mercy, either for themselves or their loved ones. They promised to change, to tithe, to serve the Church and its Master, to turn their lives around — then after the crisis ended, to revert to their old selves once again. Remind them of it and they shrug: "Did I really say that? I don't recall." Or, "I'm not so sure it really was God. I might have thought so at the time, but I've changed my mind." Perhaps you may have known somebody like that also. Perhaps, you yourself may be one of them — may it not be! Gratitude is hard to come by.

Thirteenth Day
THE FAITH OF THE MARTYRS
Matthew 10:27-33

Whatever I tell you in the dark, speak in the light; and what you hear in the ear, preach on the housetops. And do not fear those who kill the body but cannot kill the soul. But rather fear Him who is able to destroy both soul and body in hell. Are not two sparrows sold for a copper coin? And not one of them falls to the ground apart from your Father's will. But the very hairs of your head are all numbered. Do not fear therefore; you are of more value than many sparrows. Therefore whoever confesses Me before men, him I will also confess before My Father who is in heaven. But whoever denies Me before men, him I will also deny before My Father who is in heaven.'

The famous words of President Franklin Delano Roosevelt, a cripple himself, at the beginning of his presidency: "The only thing we have to fear is fear itself." Fear is the crippler of the mind and heart. It weakens and reduces the person to a shallow imitation of his or her true self. Jesus is insisting that we have no reason to be afraid of anything on the earth. Truth will ultimately conquer every lie. Courage triumphs over every intimidation. Tyrants and murderers can take our lives from us, but nobody can kill truth.

He's addressing all pastors and preachers: *What you hear in the ear, preach on the housetops.* We are to set ourselves apart, find some place far from the noise of the streets and the blare of television sets, so that we can listen to the voice of the Spirit whispering God's truth to our ear. Look at the icons of the evangelists, and note how they cock their heads to focus on heavenly sounds. But we speak mostly in churches. *On the housetops* suggests the witness from all baptized Christians, taking the message they hear in the churches out into the world where they spend the weekdays. What is that message? **Christ is risen from the dead, trampling down death by death, and upon those in the tombs bestowing life.** It's not just a hymn to sing triumphantly during the Paschal season. This announcement is the truth we live by, and for which we gladly die. With Christ alive in our hearts, we shall never die; or rather, death cannot contain us. If the last and worst enemy is death, then not only Christ but we also in Him and through Him will be snatched from death's grip and lifted up to be presented at the Throne of the Father. *Whatever I tell you in the dark, speak in the light.*

Christ is saying that there are dark moments in life, and they are precious to us. Some we look for, such as learning to love being apart from all others and alone with Him. We go off in the woods to imbibe the silence of nature, or we make a special room where we can pray in solitude. Russians had always cherished simple huts, called *pustinia,* or empty places where distractions can be lessened and the soul attuned to the voice of God. Other dark moments are chosen for us: Times of illness when we are forced to lie in bed, and after feeling natural self-pity, reflect on where we are, how we got there, and where we go from there: Back to the same way of living? Or do we alter our plans and life style?

Some dark moments we don't care to expose to anyone; yet we know that He is aware of them. When we seek out our confessor and cleanse ourselves of those dark times, we walk out into the light.

He is asking that we share with those who may benefit from our experiences what God has done for us in our darkest moments, regardless of how we got there.

Fourteenth Day
WORTHY TO SIT AT GOD'S BANQUET
Matthew 22:1-14

The kingdom of heaven is like a certain king who arranged a marriage for his son, and sent out his servants to call those who were invited to the wedding and they were not willing to come. Again he sent out other servants, saying, 'Tell those who were invited, "See, I have prepared my dinner; my oxen and fatted cattle are killed, and all things are ready. Come to the wedding."' But they made light of it and went their ways, one to his own farm, another to his business. And the rest seized his servants, treated them spitefully, and killed them. But when the king heard about it, he was furious. And he sent out his armies, destroyed those murderers, and burned up their city. Then he said to his servants, 'The wedding is ready, but those who were invited were not worthy. Therefore go into the highways, and as many as you find, invite to the wedding.' So those servants went out to the highways and gathered together all whom they found, both bad and good, and the wedding was filled with guests. But when the king came to see the guests, he saw a man who did not have on a wedding garment. So he said to him, 'Friend, how did you come in here without a wedding garment?' And he was speechless. Then the king said to the servants, 'Bind him hand and foot and take him away, and cast him into outer darkness, there will be weeping and gnashing of teeth, for many are called, but few are chosen.'

The original meaning of Christ's story of the banquet feast in God's Kingdom was an indictment of the Jews. They had been the intended guests, but they refused the invitation. God sent His Son to prepare the great wedding festival for Himself, but the chosen people chose to reject the invitation. So He went out to find others who didn't even know there was to be a banquet. Whatever they were doing otherwise, they were ordered to stop, and they were told to make themselves ready, because God would not do without a celebration party. His joy could not be complete without company.

The king is God. *He was furious.* The city He had burned was Jerusalem. Those who rejected His Son were punished. This gospel was written probably in Alexandria, Egypt, after Jerusalem had been destroyed. It gives a reason for what was a horrible incident for all, Jews and Christians.

How many baptized into Christ since then, have better things to do with their time than to celebrate with God the joy of their own salvation? How do you think He will treat those who reject, ignore, or scorn the banquet He has prepared for them? Prayer and fellowship in the Church is an obligation, a requirement they decide they can do without. Yet this is about happiness and celebration, not a tiresome duty. It isn't opposed to worldly pleasures, tending to one's home or business. It asks only that life be prioritized, and God's wishes are our first priority.

It addresses the modern illusion that God's great love will excuse all our sins. We need not dress for the occasion, means that no preparation is necessary. "Just as I am" is the slogan of contemporary America. Not so, says the Lord. As in the Russian proverb: "He came to dinner and brought his own spoon." But you cannot do that. If you come to God's great banquet expecting to celebrate with the saints, be warned. You do not set your own conditions for the party. You have a lifetime to prepare your baptismal garment, making your soul clean and pure, *without a spot or wrinkle or any such thing* (Eph. 5:27).

Fifteenth Day
WHAT IS TRUTH?
John 19:7-11

The Jews answered him, 'We have a law, and according to our law He ought to die, because He made Himself the Son of God.' When Pilate heard that saying, he was the more afraid, and went again into the Praetorium and said to Jesus, 'Where are You from?' But Jesus gave him no answer. Then Pilate said to Him, 'Are you not speaking to me? Do You not know that I have power to crucify You, and power to release You?' Jesus answered, 'You could have no power at all against Me unless it had been given you from above. Therefore the one who delivered Me to you has the greater sin.'

Pilate resented Jesus. He felt Jesus ought to show some respect. He was amazed that this carpenter and wandering rabbi was not pleading for His life, crawling on the ground, hugging his sandals, wallowing in tears, choking with sobs. But there was none of that. Jesus would not beg, not even for His life: Not to that man, despite his rank. And He doesn't condemn Pilate. Others are to blame for what happened that brought the two together. A far vaster plan is at work that the procurator cannot fathom.

Jesus knows that for all his pretensions, the Jewish religious leaders are manipulating Pilate, and this Roman doesn't like it. He didn't go in search for Jesus. He knows full well that he's no threat to the political situation. He is not a revolutionary in the conventional sense, leading some guerrilla force bent on overthrowing the administration of Rome. Pilate doesn't care a fig for Jewish laws, nor does he have a belief in God, much less show interest in what this poor wandering rabbi and former carpenter is called, or considers Himself: Son of God? What God? He wanted no part of Jewish squabbles.

What about us? Do we see with eyes like Pilate's, or like the Lord's? Can we realize ourselves as part of God's great plan, or is life merely a multiplication of innumerable accidents? Is there a pattern to our lives, or is existence merely a string of unconnected events devoid of meaning? Are we able to realize that whatever happens on our journey through the world the only real tragedy is to be deprived of God's embrace and a place in His kingdom when this phase of our existence comes to its conclusion?

But Jesus gave him no answer. Oh, the power of Christ's silence! There comes a time when words have no meaning, because the one we hoped to convince is incapable of understanding us. May it not be our fate to meet the eyes of the Lord on the day of Judgment, and to face His silence. It's a warning to those who think of the Lord as the American version of Santa Claus, somebody so good-natured as to be reckoned almost senile, who gives us what we ask for, not necessarily what we need for our salvation. Some feel that on Judgment Day, the Lord will grant a general immunity from prosecution, just as some of President Clinton's friends received some hours before he left office. But it won't happen, because it simply cannot happen. There will be those who shall make a case for their sins on earth, justifying what they did, unrepentant and even proud of their achievements. Napoleon died agonizing on why he failed in his determination to conquer all of Europe, unconcerned about the thousands of lives wasted in his wars. Who thinks that the eyes and light of the Lord will enlighten Hitler, Genghis Khan, Lenin, Stalin, Pol Pot, or all the lesser-known tyrants throughout history, and that they become remorseful, contrite, and beg forgiveness? Then again, with God all things are possible.

Sixteenth Day
NO HONOR OR RESPECT
Mark 6:1-6

Then He went out from there and came to His own country, and His disciples followed Him. And when the Sabbath had come, He began to teach in the synagogue. And many hearing Him were astonished, saying, 'Where did this Man get these things? And what wisdom is this, which is given to Him, that such mighty works are performed by His hands! Is this not the carpenter, the Son of Mary, and brother of James, Joses, Judas, and Simon? And are not his sisters here with us?' So they were offended at Him. But Jesus said to them, 'A prophet is not without honor except in his own country, among his own relatives, and in his own house.' Now He could do no mighty work there, except that He laid His hands on a few sick people and healed them. And He marveled because of their unbelief. Then He went about the villages in a circuit, teaching.

Jesus left His village a carpenter and returned a rabbi with a following of disciples. He went not to His shop, but to the synagogue to preach. His message was not welcomed. His neighbors saw only the Man who made their furniture, not the One who fashions souls. Their blindness is frightening. Without their faith He could do little.

Oh, the arrogance and snobbery! They who themselves were laborers and craftsmen looked down on Jesus for being One of them. Was this not the plan of His Father, that He would leave His rightful place at the side of the Almighty and take on human flesh? The Nazarene folk could not comprehend this subtle mystery; but they might have been proud that one of their own village had achieved such renown elsewhere in

Galilee. Were they envious, or just small-minded and biased against the possibility that One from the working class could become a famous teacher and healer?

Why did He take so long to begin His ministry? *We have a clue: Is this not the carpenter, the Son of Mary?* He had obligations to care for her, since Joseph was no longer alive. If the Orthodox Christians love her, they only imitate their Lord Jesus. The sadness is not a failure of Christ's power, but of the rejection of that spiritual grace by His townspeople. Homilies are half the responsibility of the congregation. The best pastors will fail if the parish refuses to heed their message, and if it rejects their ministry. Rather than a negative lesson, in fact, it gives hope to those of us who serve the Lord as His ordained servants. We realize that if it happened to Christ Himself, we should not always wallow in self-rejection and defeatism when something similar comes our way.

America is a wonderful nation. Those of us born here cannot appreciate its blessings as well as those who come to her shores from countries where they had been locked in a hopeless, endless life without any expectation of improvement or upward mobility. Here one can become whatever his talents, intelligence, and determination can make him or her. The story of America is an endless chain of successes from people of all races, creeds and backgrounds.

Unfortunately there are also those who lack ambition or the willingness to make the sacrifices needed to achieve their goals. They salve their hurt egos by looking for ways to tear down those who made successes of themselves. Like the Lord's neighbors they close themselves off from the joy that can come from sharing another's achievements, and in the end live in the misery they made for themselves. What will change for them even in heaven?

Seventeenth Day
ABSOLUTE TRUST IN GOD
Mark 6:7-13

And He called the twelve to Himself, and began to send them out two by two, and gave them power over unclean spirits. He commanded them to take nothing for the journey except a staff — no bag, no bread, no copper in their money belts — but to wear sandals, and not to put on two tunics. Also He said to them, 'In whatever place you enter a house, stay there till you depart from that place. And whoever will not receive you nor hear you, when you depart from there, shake off the dust under your feet as a testimony against them. Assuredly, I say to you, it will be more tolerable for Sodom and Gomorrah in the day of judgment than for that city.' So they went out and preached that people should repent. And they cast out many demons, and anointed with oil many who were sick, and healed them.

The passage requires some understanding of Palestine in the Lord's time. People then dressed in five articles of clothing: an undergarment, a headdress, a belt, sandals and an outer garment or tunic of which He insisted they have only one. He doesn't want them to provide for themselves, but to trust in the hospitality of strangers. In our times it makes little sense, because nobody feels really obligated to care for visitors to a city; however, in those days each village was expected to offer hospitality to outsiders. A visitor was not expected to ask for lodgings and food, it was the sacred duty of the townspeople to offer it to him. Jesus builds on such graciousness, and if it is refused, His disciples are to leave at once, and to *shake off the dust from under your feet.* Here Jesus uses a Hebrew law that a good Jew will shake off any Gentile dust when he returns to the Holy Land of Israel. It means that they are to treat inhospitality as an offense to decency. Leave them to their ignorance and selfishness. What does this say to us, especially when visitors come to our churches and are ignored and even worse?

True monastics, women and men, travel light. They follow the admonition of Christ, possessing little except the clothing they wear and articles of prayer. It's difficult to detach ourselves from our things. It calls for total trust in God, surrendering to Him for our provisions and the benevolence of strangers for our care. Solzhenitsyn, writing of the control that the guards in the Communist GULAG held over the prisoners noted that there is always something that can be taken away: a rope to hold up one's trousers, a spoon, paper, a stub of a pencil, even a button. Jesus tells us that true freedom means that we must always be ready to give it all up. Without any possessions we have the greatest Possession imaginable — Christ Jesus our Lord, God and Savior.

This commissioning of Christ's disciples opens another question: When does one give up trying to bring others to the Lord? Some would say: Never! Go on trying, hoping, praying for success. But evidence and this text demonstrate the futility of continued failure. We have only a certain amount of time and talent to invest in evangelizing. How can we be most effective in using our gifts? Where do we devote ourselves that will have the most advantage? Who will benefit the most? Nobody is incorrigible. Everybody is capable of changing, opening their souls to Christ, and being transformed; however, there comes a time when it seems only time and a radical change of heart will turn a cynic, or a nonbeliever, or a former believer into a new child of God.

Eighteenth Day
SHEEP WITHOUT A SHEPHERD
Mark 6:30-34

Then the apostles gathered to Jesus and told Him all things, both what they had done and what they had taught. And He said to them, 'Come aside by yourselves to a deserted place and rest a while.' For there were many coming and going, and they did not even have time to eat. So they departed to a deserted place in the boat by themselves. But the multitudes saw them departing, and many knew Him and ran there on foot from all the cities. They arrived before them and came together to Him. And Jesus, when He came out, saw a great multitude and was moved with compassion for them, because they were like sheep not having a shepherd. So He began to teach them many things.

It's the time for R & R, rest and relaxation for the company of Christ. The disciples, sent out by twos, had returned from their experience. They told Him that they had had little time to rest or even to eat, since they had been so involved with nourishing the crowds with spiritual food. So He told them that He would take them across the lake, to some place where they might find serenity and peace. But it never happened.

Several significant points are made here:

A. It's a myth that the Lord's servants have little to do between Sundays. It's a drain on one's emotions to continue without taking the time to recharge spiritual energies. Some pastors feel it unworthy of their calling to take time for unwinding and relaxing. There's no need to apologize or explain the need for restoring the inner batteries that stimulate the mind, body and soul.

B. The overwhelming desire to be near the Lord is a tribute to His supreme gifts. A healthy Church will experience the same hunger and thirst for grace. People will recognize the work and presence of Christ, imploring His ministers to distribute the spiritual aid that can come only from Jesus, through His Church. Worse than any feeling of being overworked and exhausted in doing the Lord's work, is to be ignored as void of any significance for those starved for Christ's gospel.

C. Regardless of His own or the disciples' weariness, Jesus sets as a priority the needs of the people of God who are *like sheep without a shepherd*. Like Him, His servants must be ready at a moment to set aside their own plans, to postpone rest for the sake of the demands which are set before them.

Like sheep without a shepherd is a phrase used by an actual shepherd, Moses, who knew all about lost and wandering sheep (Num. 27:17). Moses knew his days on earth were drawing to a close, so he prayed that the Almighty would send somebody in his place capable and worthy to continue his ministry over the people. It's not by accident, then, that the successor of Moses was Joshua, a name translated in the Greek Bible used in Jesus' time as *Jesus*. Those with "eyes to see" would have read that while Moses led the children of Israel to the boundary of the Promised Land, Joshua guided them in. The second Joshua, our Lord Jesus Christ, is leading us through this present wilderness and into the land of ultimate promise, the kingdom of His heavenly Father.

Nineteenth Day
THE ARK OF THE NEW COVENANT
Mark 6:45-53

Immediately He made His disciples get into the boat and go before Him to the other side, to Bethsaida, while He sent the multitude away. And when He had sent them away, He departed to the mountain to pray. Now when evening came, the boat was in the middle of the sea, and He was alone on the land. Then He saw them straining at rowing, for the wind was against them. Now about the fourth watch of the night He came to them, walking on the sea, and would have passed them by. And when they saw Him walking on the sea, they supposed it was a ghost, and cried out; for they all saw Him and were troubled. But immediately He talked with them and said to them, 'Be of good cheer! It is I, do not be afraid.' Then He went up into the boat to them, and the wind ceased. And they were greatly amazed in themselves beyond measure, and marveled. For they had not understood about the loaves, because their heart was hardened.

A crisis was just about to begin, and it had to do with the multiplication of loaves in the wilderness. People were clamoring for a leader who would gather his forces and raise an army that could overthrow the Roman administration. This is the meaning of the reference to loaves: *They had not understood about the loaves.* Bread in the wilderness should have reminded them of the manna which the Lord provided to those with Moses. The crowds wanted to proclaim Jesus their king, and He would have none of it. Their excitement was a danger to His ministry, and it's why He ordered the disciples to leave by the boat and cross the sea while He stayed to dismiss the crowd.

Two storms rage in this episode. The political and religious authorities are rising all around Jesus, like waves before a hurricane. Besides, some fanatics want Him to take the role of liberator, raising an army against the Roman occupation. He must be apart from everyone including His disciples. He takes refuge from that emotional turbulence in prayer. He sends a signal to all of His followers — here is the only sure way to establish order and stability in a troubled heart.

But as He had forsaken the planned rest for the disciples when the crowds gathered and pleaded for His attention, so here He postponed prayer when He realized that the apostles were in dire straits on the sea. *The fourth watch* is 3 a.m. They are about four miles out on the water. He went out to help them.

On another level of understanding, this incident gives hope and meaning to our storms of life. The boat is the Holy Church, the ark of the New Testament floating on the sea of life. Whatever tempests may rage in our lives, as long as Christ is in our hearts and we in His Church, everything will turn out right. However, when those inside take charge and do so without representing the Lord, ignoring His presence, failing to open themselves to Him in prayer, then the storms are not just outside. The ship is in danger of sinking. Jesus Christ is the sole Pilot. This fundamental truth is basic to the Orthodox Church. When one gazes upward into the ceilings of most Orthodox Churches, one should be gazing at Christ's icon and being reminded that those below in the nave (a naval term) are at peace, because the same Christ who walked across the sea to pacify the waters and comfort His disciples is both at the right hand of the Father, and at the same time watching over those whom He loves.

Twentieth Day
STAND FIRM TO THE END
Matthew 24:3-13

Now as He sat on the Mount of Olives, the disciples came to Him privately, saying, 'Tell us, when will these things be? And what will be the sign of Your coming, and of the end of the age?' And Jesus answered and said to them, 'Take heed that no one deceives you. For many will come in My name saying, "I am the Christ," and will deceive many. And you will hear of wars, and rumors of wars. See that you are not troubled, for all these things must come to pass, but the end is not yet. For nation will rise against nation, and kingdom against kingdom, and there will be famines, pestilences, and earthquakes in various places. All these are the beginning of sorrows. Then they will deliver you up to tribulation and kill you, and you will be hated by all nations for My name's sake. And then many will be offended, will betray one another and will hate one another. Then many false prophets will rise up and deceive many. And because lawlessness will abound, the love of many will grow cold. But he who endures to the end shall be saved.'

Take heed that no one deceives you. How I would like to remind so many of our own pious believers of this warning, who are taken in by the many sectarians who persist in their arrogant ignorance, forming their own charts and graphs forcing Bible texts to conform to their preconceived ideas of the end of the world.

He who endures to the end will be saved. How often I've used this sentence as the only sedative I could offer to somebody whose spiritual agony was almost too much to tolerate: those in miserable marriages who remain in the home for the sake of the children; others who endure physical sufferings, victims of a disease for which our medical science has yet to discover a cure, or persons who realize they are dying by days and degrees, looking to the Kingdom yet as humans having natural fears, dreading the unknown passage from this world. It's vital that those in such severe conditions of life draw upon their faith and pray that the Spirit of God will make up whatever is lacking. I remember John, a Marlboro Man look-like who at the age of twenty-five contracted muscular dystrophy, which slowly sapped his strength and physical functions until he would pass away seventeen years later. He had been a wrestler, moving to the state championship finals. I asked him if he ever felt sorry for his plight. He told me that quite the contrary, he was happy to have been afflicted with that terminal illness. He said that as a wrestler he first would pray for his opponent and his own safety through the match. Then he began praying only for himself. As he continued to win matches his smugness grew, and he entertained a sinful thought: "Why am I praying to God? It's not He but I who am out there on the mat." Only when he was bedfast did he have the time to reflect on his arrogance and sinful pride. In losing his physical body he regained his precious soul. *The love of many will grow cold;* pray God it not be their own love. They imbibe the love of those who care for them and do their best to respond in kind; but more than any virtue they require hope, for without it they die even before they are pronounced dead. It's imperative that we monitor one another's devotion to the Lord, just as during a severe winter we encourage our relatives and friends to stay warm and take precautions against the cold. We can warm the cold hearts and inspire each other with the fire of Christ, if we truly believe the words: "Let us love one another that with one mind and one heart we may confess Father, Son, and Holy Spirit, the Trinity one in essence and undivided."

Twenty-first Day
THE GREATEST COMMANDMENT
Matthew 22:34-46

But when the Pharisees heard that He had silenced the Sadducees, they gathered together. Then one of them, a lawyer, asked Him a question, testing Him and saying, 'Teacher, which is the greatest commandment in the law?' Jesus said to him, 'You shall love the Lord your God with all your heart, with all your soul, and with all your mind. This is the first and great commandment. And the second is like it: You shall love your neighbor as yourself. On these two commandments hang all the law and Prophets.'

Jesus *silenced the Sadducees* when they taunted him over a hypothetical problem. A woman married the brother of her dead husband, and then when he died, she married another brother, going through seven brothers. Whose wife would she be in heaven? Jesus demolished their argument, based on equating this lifetime with eternity. Surely they should know that heaven is not a continuation of life as we know it. Life in the beyond is not to be compared with this world.

What is religion all about? This is what Jesus is explaining. One theologian quite popular in the last century, Paul Tillich, trying to widen the definition of religion said it is a person's "ultimate concern." The artist's religion is his painting, the composer's his music, the architect's his building. This is using the term *religion* beyond the boundaries of theology. Jesus makes clear the true meaning of religion: Ultimate love of God, and love for all humanity. And He places them in proper perspective.

You must love God with everything that is within you. St. Augustine wrote, "Love God; then do as you please." If a person does just that and thinks through the implications, he cannot make an error, for he will thereby love everything else that God has created. Some, however, find a way to base their beliefs on God, and then appoint themselves His defense attorney. They make a lifetime of hating what they perceive as variation from their definition of God. The infamous Inquisition of the Middle Ages was such a distortion of faith. We all know the type who has enough religion to hate what God hates, but cannot find it within their hearts to love what He loves.

Another opposite extreme is to reject a deity who would allow suffering on earth. The famous Dostoevsky novel *Brothers Karamazov* takes up this theme. Ivan is an atheist. He cannot make himself believe in a God who would permit innocent suffering to happen. Why does God permit men to torture others, or to bring agony to children? Such a God is either impotent or unconcerned. Suffering is indeed a deep mystery. Jesus Himself does not offer any explanation other than to share the suffering of mankind on the Cross. Love is always an ongoing challenge. Obstacles arise on the journey through life that cause us to pause at times and measure the love we say we have for others.

The Sadducees based their religion on ritual observances, formulas of prayer and sacrifices they felt pleased the Lord. But David's prayer reminds us: "You do not desire sacrifice, else I would give it; *You do not delight in burnt offerings. The sacrifices to God are a broken spirit; a broken and a contrite heart You will not despise* (Psa. 51:16). The Pharisees built their faith on observance of laws. They made a religion of legalism, following rules that they imposed on others, harnessing God's freedom into a system. Jesus offers a faith that transcends all human limits to His grace and glory.

Twenty-Second Day
THE TEMPTATION
Luke 4:1-4

Then Jesus, being filled with the Holy Spirit, returned from the Jordan and was led by the Spirit into the wilderness, being tempted for forty days by the devil. And in those days He ate nothing, and afterward when they had ended, He was hungry. And the devil said to Him, 'If You are the Son of God, command this stone to become bread.' But Jesus answered him, 'It is written: Man shall not live by bread alone, but by every word of God.'

We each deal with problems and conflicts in ways consistent with our personalities. Some face them aggressively, looking to do battle with an opponent. Another will try persuasion. A third will plead and beg for mercy. Jesus is about to set forth on His movement to change the hearts of all people by returning us to His Father in heaven. He refuses to use physical force, and He will not utilize patriotism for His purposes. Unlike the military leaders such as Napoleon, who led thousands to their death in the name of glory and France, Jesus will not reduce His goal or lower His sights to such human devices. His way is the way of suffering and the cross.

We find Him hungry to the point of starvation. "You are God's Son," the devil whispers, "Surely He would want you change one of the loaf- size stones into bread and feed yourself." Jesus refuses to alter the way things are, even in a fallen world, and certainly not for His own sake. It's not for Him to transform the substance of creation, but to convert the hearts of the men and women in the world.

Note also that Jesus does not enter into a discussion with the devil. He refers to the Holy Bible and allows the Spirit of God to direct His own thoughts. If Christ, who was able to overwhelm the best Pharisees and Sadducees by persuasion chooses not to debate the devil, how much more should we not dialogue with the workers of evil, but turn instead to the Bible for our spiritual sustenance.

When we pray: *Give us this day our daily bread,* we don't mean the food we purchase from the bakery. Actually, most of us Americans do not know the meaning of hunger. Listen to a teenager at a restaurant say: "I'm starving," and you realize how paltry are words, how meaningless to so privileged a people as we are. What we plead for in our prayer is to be nourished with the food of the Kingdom. Give us, Lord, what only You can offer; that is, the food that never fills us, but which by our consuming it, only whets our appetites for more of the same. Give us that which we never need to diet or exercise from after having eaten.

The Bread of Life is Christ Himself. We are uniting ourselves with holiness when we receive Holy Communion. How can we ever become properly prepared for such a feast? Teach me, Lord: What must I do in order to dress in proper attire, and present myself at Your table with the attitude and disposition that will make You pleased with me? When I consider the awesome company I keep there — the saints of all the ages who have been pleasing to You, "the apostles, prophets preachers, martyrs, confessors, saints," commemorated immediately following the consecration of the Holy Gifts, how dare I feel myself worthy to be there?

Twenty-Third Day
WORSHIP THE LORD YOUR GOD
Luke 4:5-13

Then the devil, taking Him upon a high mountain, showed Him all the kingdoms of the world in a moment of time. And the devil said to Him, 'All this authority I will give You, and their glory, for this has been delivered to me, and I give it to whomever I wish. Therefore if You will worship before me, all will be Yours.' And Jesus answered and said to him, 'Get behind Me, Satan! For it is written, You shall worship the Lord your God, and Him only you shall serve.' Then he brought Him to Jerusalem, set Him on the pinnacle of the temple, and said to Him, 'If You are the Son of God, throw Yourself down from here. For it is written: "He shall give His angels charge over you, to keep you," and "In their hands they shall bear you up, lest you dash your foot against a stone."' And Jesus answered and said to him, 'It has been said, "You shall not tempt the Lord your God."' Now when the devil had ended every temptation, he departed from Him until an opportune time.

Technically Satan is not lying, but he is not telling all the truth. God did not really give him the world as a gift; however, God allows sin to find a place in the hearts of human beings, both individuals and leaders of the nations of the earth. Satan shows himself for what he is; that is, the ultimate liar and deceiver. As he once whispered to Eve that she would not die, but she would be like God, knowing good and evil (Gen. 3:5), so he pretends to have all the power and glory of every earthly civilization, and he offers it to Jesus. This is a temptation to make a bargain with the world as it is. People are simple creatures, Satan says. Don't try to give them what they cannot understand and may not want. Don't tell them that they are living in sin and must repent and change their entire way of living. They are quite satisfied with any slight improvement in their lives. They understand they will die. They accept their limitations. They're confused with the promise of something more. They have been convinced by their scientists and self-styled intellectuals that basically they are little more than complicated animals, the top of the food chain, accidents of destiny. Why complicate them with a promise of everlasting life and a bond of union with the heavenly Father? Give them what they want, not what they need. Lower your standards. All those arguments Satan used against Jesus, and they are the same statements made today, with a great deal more success.

Jesus will have none of it. He came to restore God's plan on the earth, and nothing less will do. He brought salvation, peace, and life everlasting to mankind. He will not be content with a temporary era of good feelings and an array of promises that politicians spout at election time. Even if He had been able to lead a revolution and overthrow the bonds of Roman domination in Palestine, that would not be worthy of the Son of God, since Israel had long been just another nation on the earth, like any other. They had lost the vision announced by the prophet Isaiah: *I am about to create Jerusalem as a joy, and its people as a delight* (65:19). Jesus knew that the Jerusalem of Isaiah was no more. He offered a New Jerusalem coming down from heaven, whose citizens we are.

Now when the devil had ended every temptation, he departed from Him until an opportune time. Oh, he'd be back. He would use Simon Peter to tempt Jesus with the same clever ruse. He succeeded in stealing Judas Iscariot. And if the devil was a formidable opponent of the Son of God, how cautious must we be to keep ourselves from his influence and control.

Twenty-Fourth Day
JESUS AND THE UNCLEAN DEMON
Luke 4:31-37

Then He went down to Capernaum, a city of Galilee, and was teaching them on the Sabbaths. And they were astonished at His teaching, for His word was with authority. Now in the synagogue there was a man who had a spirit of an unclean demon. And he cried out with a loud voice, saying, 'Let us alone! What have we to do with You, Jesus of Nazareth? Did You come to destroy us? I know who You are — the Holy One of God!' But Jesus rebuked him, saying, 'Be quiet, and come out of him!' And when the demon had thrown him in their midst, it came out of him and did not hurt him. Then they were all amazed and spoke among themselves, saying, 'What a word this is! For with authority and power He commands the unclean spirits, and they come out.' And the report about Him went out into every place in the surrounding region.

His word was with authority. The rabbis and scribes would quote the Bible to prove their message. Jesus did not refer to Moses, but let the truth of His own words speak for themselves; after all, He is the Word of God, and through Him was grace revealed to Moses and the prophets. His authority extended to angels and demons. We imagine the reverent silence in the Capernaum synagogue broken by a man screaming and yelling, creating a scene. A demon spoke within the man, pleading with Jesus to go away and leave him alone. He knew who Jesus really was, an identity missed by most of the ordinary folks. What are we to make of it?

We must ignore two extremes: First, to be frightened of demons is wrong. Jesus came to liberate us from all fear, including that of unseen spirits. Second, to do as many in our society, and consider demons to be a superstition from the past. Modern people, even Christians, suggest that Jesus was patronizing the people of His time by healing their mental illnesses, letting them go on thinking the afflicted were possessed by demons. Luke the physician especially distinguishes demonic possession from normal illnesses, including insanity, leprosy, deafness, blindness and the like. Demon-possession is neither a mental nor a physical ailment. It's an affliction more prevalent during Christ's ministry than in the Old Testament or after Pentecost, mainly because He came specifically to do battle with the immaterial forces of evil. He came to earth like a hunter stalking a savage animal in a dark cave, bearing a flaming torch to back the beast into the recesses of darkness, and we following Him have nothing to fear as long as we are with Him or not far behind Him, and He with us.

We should neither fear nor respect the devil; however, we must not ignore his presence within our lives and our society. Especially to those who are committed to a change of attitude to God and themselves, I offer a word of caution. Throughout my priesthood I've celebrated the conversion of heart among so many who either had a lukewarm relationship with Christ, or never knew Him at all. When they discover the treasures of the Orthodox Church, they dive into them like pirates opening a chest of precious jewels on a desert island. Suddenly everything in their lives takes on a new meaning. They pray through the day and late into the night. Television, motion pictures, entertainment lose their interest. They read the church fathers and every spiritual book they can afford. They make their homes and apartments mini-chapels, with icons, crosses, Bibles in each room. Then Satan comes to call. That's when the real challenge begins.

Twenty-Fifth Day
THE SPIRIT OF PETER'S MOTHER-IN-LAW
Luke 4:38-39

Now He arose from the synagogue and entered Simon's house. But Simon's wife's mother was sick with a high fever, and they made request of Him concerning her. So He stood over her and rebuked the fever, and it left her. And immediately she arose and served them.

A rather minor miracle of healing, in contrast to the expulsion of demons, giving sight to the blind, hearing to the deaf, not to mention raising the dead; yet we have a portrait of life so touching that we're glad that it had been recorded in the holy Bible. When we think of St. Peter on an icon he's either alone or with another apostle. We hardly think of him as a family man with a wife, children and a mother-in-law in his home. How proud he must have been to show them off before his new friend and master.

But the center of the little episode is really the woman who rose from her bed and refused to let her daughter or anybody else steal her place as mistress of the kitchen and hostess of the evening meal. The Church is often accused of being patriarchal. If only it were known that it is the women who have been the backbone and main support of Christ's Church through the centuries. A Communist official once chided an Orthodox archbishop in the latter stages of atheism in Russia: "Your cult is sustained and kept alive by old women. Once they go to their graves, your vaunted institution will die." The archbishop replied: "You know, sir, that we have survived Communism for more than sixty years, and we've raised quite a number of old women in that time."

Solzhenitsyn in searching for heroes who stood up to the Communists wrote of one such elderly woman imprisoned and questioned by ruthless interrogators. "We know that a bishop was at your apartment. We want to know who had housed him before that, and to whom he went when he left you. If you won't tell us we'll kill you." The brave soul said, "It wasn't a bishop. He was the Metropolitan! Can you imagine, and in my humble apartment! And you won't kill me because you will be punished, since I will not be able to be of service to you. But I refuse to tell you what you wish. I have no fear of you." Ask any priest the source of spirituality in the parish, which are the major supporters, or where he can go to find the heart of the community. He will usually mention women. I find them braver in a general way, more capable of dealing with grief, heartaches, and the agony that comes to us all at some time or another in this world. It's a mystery to me why so many women I have known are able to face life honestly, understanding the suffering of Christ as something to share and not try avoiding, then go on with their prayers and devotion during and following their greatest tragedies. And I, a male, a priest, called "Father," feel that I'm at my best when I am doing God's work by training which women appear to do instinctively; that is, gentling others, tending to their spiritual needs, comforting and soothing them in trauma times.

Lord, I thank You for having shared this lifetime with so many like the mother-in-law of St. Peter. I've seen them in the parish of my childhood, in the cathedral where I had first served You, and here in this present church. They are so inspirational in their humility and devotion to You. They need no titles or honors, they demand nothing from You or the Church, but only the privilege of offering their lives to You.

Twenty-Sixth Day
THE GREAT CATCH OF FISH
Luke 5:1-11

So it was, as the multitude pressed about Him to hear the word of God, that He stood by the Lake of Gennesaret, and saw two boats standing by the lake, but the fishermen had gone from them and were washing their nets. Then He got into one of the boats, which was Simon's, and asked him to put out a little from the land. And he sat down and taught the multitudes from the boat. When He had stopped speaking, He said to Simon, 'Launch out into the deep and let down your nets for a catch.' But Simon answered and said to Him, 'Master, we have toiled all night and caught nothing; nevertheless at Your word I will let down the net.' And when they had done this, they caught a great number of fish, and their net was breaking. So they signaled to their partners in the other boat to come and help them. And they came and filled both the boats, so that they began to sink. When Simon Peter saw it, he fell down at Jesus' knees saying, 'Depart from me for I am a sinful man, O Lord.'

Simon Peter turns from a hearer to a doer. Imagine his boat serving as a primitive church. He and his fellows had just returned from an exhausting night's fishing. They are not just weary; they are a bit discouraged. As he listens to Jesus explaining the wonders of God and a world that is hidden from ordinary eyes, suddenly the Lord turns to him and says that He would like Simon to go back out into the sea. There are fish out there that he missed catching. Was it a test? Quite! Impulsive Simon Peter must have thought: What can He teach me about fishing, I who had been doing this all my life? Besides, he wanted only to be lulled by comforting words about God, not ordered to return to the sea.

It explains something about Jesus. His sermon was a show and tell lesson. He told Simon what He expected, and when the disciple obeyed, then He showed him where the fish were. Our Lord is the God who acts, and He does so through us. True Christianity is not for spectators. The world is a field, we are in a contest, and every one of us is a player. Then Simon Peter says: *Depart from me, for I am a sinful man, O Lord!* At another occasion he was not averse to rebuking Jesus (Matt. 16:23). Here he realizes that this Teacher is no ordinary human being. His Lord is of one essence with the Lord Almighty. Here is a moment in his lifetime that he will never forget. May each of us have something similar happen to us in our days on this earth.

To understand what happened to Peter that day is to grasp the essential difference between true, or Orthodox Christianity and all other varieties. At first, Peter loved, honored, and was ready to obey Jesus. He saw Him as a special human being, which many Christians and even non-Christians would agree with. But until the net of Christ's true nature caught him, recognizing God at work in Him, he was only an admirer. In time Peter would understand much more about Christ; but at the moment he saw God in Him. The Orthodox Church never tires of explaining the inexplicable mystery — Jesus Christ is the only-begotten, unique Son of God, **true God of true God,** as the Creed proclaims. God alone is capable of saving us from sin and death. Because Christ is God, it is not only possible, salvation has become the supreme goal of our lives.

Twenty-Seventh Day
THE THINGS THAT CAN DEFILE A PERSON
Mark 7:14-23

When He had called all the multitude to Himself, He said to them, 'Hear Me, everyone, and understand. There is nothing that enters a man from outside which can defile him; but the things which come out of him, those are the things that defile a man. If anyone has ears to hear, let him hear!' When He had entered a house away from the crowd, his disciples asked Him concerning the parable. So He said to them, 'Are you thus without understanding also? Do you not perceive that whatever enters a man from outside cannot defile him, because it does not enter his heart but his stomach, and is eliminated, thus purifying all foods?' And He said, 'What comes out of a man, that defiles a man. For from within, out of the heart of men, proceed evil thoughts, adulteries, fornications, murders, thefts, covetousness, wickedness, deceit, lewdness, an evil eye, blasphemy, pride, foolishness. All these evil things come from within and defile a man.'

In a single phrase, Jesus deals with the ceremonial law of kosher foods that are part of the Hebrew faith then and now. *There is nothing that enters a person from outside which can defile him.* All foods are clean and can be eaten. Put in other terms, it is not **things** that are either clean or unclean; it is **persons** who are able to defile themselves by their deeds and thoughts. It's not what goes into one's body, but what proceeds from his or her heart. It took a bold Person to make so startling a statement to His own people. Their religion is based on ritual foods and specific customs with laws for every situation and activity. He centers faith elsewhere — in the human soul.

Then He itemizes the various sins that come from a defiled heart. Just as a person may not be aware of aromas in his own living quarters, whereas a visitor from the fresh outdoors may notice them, so too the pure, wholesome, innocent heart of our Lord Jesus is more sensitive to the various human defilements than others such as we:

Evil thoughts head the list. No sinful act occurs without first an evil thought. Before Eve tempted Adam, before they tasted the forbidden fruit, there was the wicked idea planted by Satan. The Orthodox Christian at baptism receives the "seal of the gift of the Holy Spirit." He or she is marked at every portal of the senses, with Holy Myrrh which is like a guardian angel set as a guard to be on the lookout for whatever spiritual virus may enter; but it is from within the mind that the danger lies. *Adulteries* is plural, meaning all sorts of sexual immorality, *fornication* being one form. *Murders, thefts, covetousness, wickedness, deceit* all are unfortunately rather self-explanatory. *Covetousness* is made from two Greek words that mean "wanting to have more." It's a curse that in our day is taken to be normal for many. Professional athletes paid obscene salaries that they couldn't possibly spend in a lifetime are ever on the lookout for more money. It's truly a spiritual disease, the insatiable lust not just for things, but for power and sexual prowess, which never leave one content or fulfilled. Such persons seek satisfaction in things, not in the Lord God. The *evil eye* is the direct translation from the Greek, meaning envy. It comes from a person who would curse another's good fortune if he could. We know such persons who cannot enjoy another's happiness without finding some way to criticize or demean the other. Lord bless us, we find them even in the Church among the family of Christ. Oddly, the Lord puts pride near the end of His list. Later, many church fathers placed it at the top of their catalogs. Christ ends with the same phrase with which He had begun, so that nobody could miss His point: *All these evil things come from within and defile a man."*

Twenty-Eighth Day
THE FAITH OF A GENTILE WOMAN
Mark 7:24-30

From there He arose and went to the region of Tyre and Sidon. And He entered a house and wanted no one to know it, but He could not be hidden. For a woman whose young daughter had an unclean spirit heard about Him, and she came and fell at His feet. The woman was a Greek, a Syro-Phoenician by birth, and she kept asking Him to cast the demon out of her daughter. But Jesus said to her, 'Let the children be filled first, for it is not good to take the children's bread and throw it to the little dogs.' And she answered and said to Him, 'Yes, Lord, yet even the little dogs under the table eat from the children's crumbs.' Then He said to her, 'For this saying go your way; the demon has gone out of your daughter.' And when she came home to her house she found the demon gone out and her daughter lying on the bed.

He could not be hidden.

Of course not! Is this not the Light of the world? How then can He be put under a bushel? He came to be *a light to enlighten the Gentiles, and the glory of His people, Israel.* Well, He accomplished the first part. When He made His grand entrance into Jerusalem on the day we call now Palm Sunday, he was willing to let His light shine openly: "Some of the Pharisees in the crowd said to Him, *"Teacher, order your disciples to stop."* He answered, *"I tell you, if these were silent, the stones would shout out"* (Luke 19:39). Just before this we learned that Jesus had abolished the distinction between clean and unclean foods. Here He is rubbing out the border between Jew and Gentile. It helps explain why He left the territory of Israel proper. Actually these seaport cities had been given to the tribe of Asher, however, they were not able to dominate the region. So many of its inhabitants were Gentiles of various ethnic backgrounds.

Certainly He hasn't given up on transforming His own people, although another reason for His being so far off is to escape, at least for a while, the forces that had been oppressing Him. He broke the strict laws of the Pharisees and scribes; therefore they were set on getting rid of Him. King Herod must have seen Him as a potential troublemaker, possibly stirring up the crowds. His own townspeople had nothing to do with Him. He could use a break, a time for reflection and preparation before He would deal with His enemies head-on.

He wasn't up to helping the woman with her daughter's ailment. Perhaps a wide range of people accosted him, and He hoped to pass through incognito. He told her that His major concern was for His own people. He didn't reject her. We can imagine Him smiling when He said that the children's food ought not to be thrown to the puppies. But He liked the wit of the lady who came back with a witticism of her own: *even the little dogs . . . eat from the children's crumbs.* For us it's a lesson in humility, not only in this world but in the next, where we Americans who have had so much in our lifetimes and do so little with it will be in the presence of the martyrs, missionaries and saints of ages past whose entire lives were a matter of struggling to bear witness to Christ while barely being able to stave off starvation, danger, persecution, homelessness, and other challenges.

Twenty-Ninth Day
THE HEALING OF A DEAF MAN
Mark 7:31-37

Again, departing from the region of Tyre and Sidon, He came through the midst of the region of Decapolis to the sea of Galilee. Then they brought to Him one who was deaf and had an impediment in his speech, and they begged Him to put His hand on him. And He took him aside from the multitude, and put His fingers in his ears, and He spat and touched his tongue. Then, looking up to heaven, He sighed and said to him, Ephphatha, *that is, 'Be opened.' Immediately his ears were opened and the impediment of his tongue was loosed and he spoke plainly. Then He commanded them that they should tell no one; but the more He commanded them, the more widely they proclaimed it. And they were astonished beyond measure, saying, 'He has done all things well. He makes both the deaf to hear and the mute to speak.'*

How poignant is the manner in which our Lord dealt with the deaf man. *He took him aside from the multitude.* Anyone with a physical impairment is sensitive to the stares and comments of others. They take any whispers personally even when they aren't referring to them. It wasn't the Lord's purpose to make a public spectacle of His healing powers. The poor man disliked crowds. He had learned how to live in the chamber of his own seclusion. So many make the same sad adjustment. They find a place for themselves on the periphery of family and society, spending the brief allotment of life shut off and alone, trying to convince themselves that they prefer living that way. Jesus recognized the condition and was sensitive to his feelings. He took him aside, touching him gently at the places that caused his shyness and reticence.

Think of the difference from some of the television healers who in Christ's Name use the opportunity to put on a curative display. The Orthodox Christian custom of healing is to have several priests, preferably seven, praying over the sick, culminating in the holding of the open Gospels over their heads, to make it evident that it is Christ Himself in the presence of *two or three gathered in* His *Name* rather than one spiritual superstar that brings the healing to the afflicted.

What He does next is to demonstrate to the deaf man His intentions and the method of healing He will employ. *He put His fingers in his ears* in order that the man would not be frightened or startled. *He spat and touched his tongue.* Spittle was considered to have healing properties. To us it may appear unsanitary; but to the man it would have been a welcome sign that indeed he would be cured of his stammer. They go together, deafness and a speech impediment, since the deaf had never heard the sound of others' voices, much less his own. How wonderful then that the man would not have to suffer from being able to hear, yet unable to form words like normal persons. Some feel that the man may have suffered from spasms of the facial muscles, which is another reason why Jesus would have wanted to take him aside privately to work the miracle.

Then He commanded them that they should tell no one. It's not so much a matter of modesty, although He wasn't averse to healing in public places. Rather, He would prefer to hold off the time when He would be in the center of the storm raging around His person, and He felt that He had so much more to accomplish before the long fateful journey from Galilee to Jerusalem and the cross.

Thirtieth Day
FEEDING FOUR THOUSAND
Mark 8:1-10

In those days, the multitude being very great and having nothing to eat, Jesus called His disciples to Him and said to them, 'I have compassion on the multitude, because they have now continued with me three days and have nothing to eat. And if I send them away hungry to their own houses, they will faint on the way; for some of them have come from afar.' Then His disciples answered Him, 'How can one satisfy these people with bread here in the wilderness?' He asked them, 'How many loaves do you have?' And they said, 'Seven.' So He commanded the multitude to sit down on the ground. And He took the seven loaves and gave thanks, broke them and gave them to His disciples to set before them, and they set them before the multitude. They also had a few small fish; and having blessed them He said to set them also before them. So they ate and were filled, and they took up seven large baskets of leftover fragments. Now those who had eaten were about four thousand. And He sent them away, immediately got into the boat with His disciples, and came to the region of Dalmanutha.

We might note the thanksgiving of the Lord over the loaves, then the blessing over the fish before the food was distributed. Here was a mixed crowd. Earlier across the lake He had performed a similar miracle of five loaves and two fish, feeding five thousand. Most of them were Jews who were familiar with their custom of prayers at the breaking of bread. Now in an uncounted crowd, many of whom were strangers and Gentiles, it seems that Jesus was teaching them that it is always proper to give thanks to God before each meal.

We might term this a three-day retreat. Many of the crowd came from villages and towns in the area, but others had traveled quite a distance, and by the time they would get home they would be famished or worse. *I have compassion on the multitude.* A key feature of Christ's personality is His tender heart, a soul that agonizes over the sins, sickness and weaknesses He finds among the people on earth. When He told Philip who asked to see the Father in heaven, *Have I been so long with you, Philip, and you still don't know Me? Whoever has seen Me has seen the Father* (John 14:9), we are to understand that the same characteristic compassion and consideration for others is shared by Father and Son. Otherwise our ongoing pleas for His mercy would be of no avail.

If the crowds were exhausted after being with Him and listening to His teachings for three long days, imagine how He must have felt! Yet His concern is not for Himself, but for the welfare of those with Him. Among the most brutal, insensitive phrases in society is: "I could care less!" Those who use it do so without embarrassment. Yet some even have the audacity to call themselves by Christ's Name. To be a Christian is to be Christlike: to have His attitudes and attributes on display for the world to see and emulate. The next part of the story is that He did more than have compassion on the multitude. He did something about it. Others would shrug their shoulders and walk away from the situation. As in the Chinese proverb: "That's no problem. That's impossible." But Jesus would not walk away and leave the hungry masses to fend for themselves.

The third aspect is that the meal was shared. Of course it was a miracle that could cause seven loaves and several fish to make do for four thousand persons; but it was helped along by the fact that everybody took just a bit and not one gorged himself without caring about their neighbor. Would that we all had a similar concern for the welfare of others.

Thirty-first Day
WHO DO MEN SAY THAT I AM?
Mark 8 :27-30

Now Jesus and His disciples went out to the towns of Caesarea Philippi; and on the road He asked His disciples, saying to them, 'Who do men say that I am?' So they answered, 'John the Baptist; but some say, Elijah; and others, one of the prophets.' He said to them, 'But who do you say that I am?' Peter answered and said to Him, 'You are the Christ.' Then He strictly warned them that they should tell no one about Him.

Unlike a normal rabbi located in a city where he can be visited, Jesus was homeless. He was not accepted in His hometown. He and His disciples are at an interesting location — a place where a variety of deities had a presence. This region of Banias or Pannias we know from Matthew's gospel is named for the pagan god Pan. Here Romans worshipped Caesar as a deity. Here is the center of Mark's gospel. Up to this time Jesus had been a person possessing extraordinary spiritual powers that astonished His fellow Jews and caused the Roman rulers to wonder where His authority and wisdom came from. Still, His true dignity remained hidden to all. Because He associated with sinners and disregarded the strict rules and observances of the religious leaders, they could only imagine that His power came from the demons. Even when He expelled demons, it still provoked only criticism from the bystanders. Even His disciples could find no category in which to place Him. He preached repentance like John the Baptist and maybe even looked like him, since they were related. He warned not to depend on God's protection for the temple, like Jeremiah. But no definition quite encompassed the whole person of Jesus.

The people all had their own opinions about Him. Nobody could quite classify Him, though they tried mightily. He was a rabbi, yet untrained by any known scholar. He had a thorough grasp of the Bible, but he never used Moses or one of the prophets to justify His comments. As they noted, and as He stunned the professional teachers *He spoke with His own authority.* Not by accident did He take His followers on a mountain, since that's where the Almighty first confronted Moses. If it still was not clear, He made a point of starting His teachings: *It is written* . . . adding: *but I say to you* . . . To this day He remains a controversial figure. *I came to bring . . . a sword.* That sword divides all mankind into those who acknowledge Him to be the Son of God, and all the others. *But who do you say that I am?*, He asked His disciples. Each of us — though we are baptized in His name and buried with Him in baptism, so that we may be raised with Him on the last day — must also personally address that question. The last two words of the question give a hint: *I am.* This is the Name that the Almighty told to Moses on Mt. Sinai (Ex. 3: 14). It's inscribed in every icon of Christ. If we say that He is the Son of God, what are the implications for us? St. Peter speaks on behalf of every disciple with the insight given to him through the Holy Spirit: *You are the Christ* (or, in Hebrew, **Messiah**). Here is a phrase worthy of nourishing our minds and souls through contemplation. It makes Christianity different from all other religions of mankind. It tells us that God, while remaining above and beyond all creation, transcending every possibility to comprehend who He is, nevertheless came to earth living and dwelling among us. What love He must have for us: What love He must expect from us!

Thirty-second Day
JESUS PREDICTS HIS PASSION
Mark 8:31-34

And He began to teach them that the Son of Man must suffer many things, and be rejected by the elders and chief priests and scribes, and be killed, and after three days rise again. He spoke this word openly. Then Peter took Him aside and began to rebuke Him. But when He had turned around and looked at His disciples, He rebuked Peter, saying, 'Get behind Me, Satan! For you are not mindful of the things of God, but the things of men.'

Understand that the apostles had a fixed comprehension of what it would be "When Messiah comes," in the joyous expression of the Jewish people. To them it meant celebration, vindication of the eras of suffering of their nation, a time for happiness and blessings. Remember Christ's own mother: when she heard that through her the Messiah was coming, she could barely contain herself, praising God in song:

> *He has brought down the mighty from their thrones,*
>   *and lifted up the lowly;*
> *He has filled the hungry with good things,*
>   *and sent the rich away empty.*   –Luke 1:52

What Jesus was telling them was incomprehensible. It was incredible that He would suffer, be rejected, and put to death. Peter who had spoken for them in the Spirit, proclaiming Jesus to be the Christ, now speaks once again — this time in the confusion of his heart. Was it audacious to dare talk to the

Lord in such a familiar manner? Probably. But they had been together for so long a time that he must have felt that it ought to be acceptable. Jesus was a humble teacher, not putting on airs or demanding the respect due Him as rabbi. Look how harshly He rebuts Peter: *Get behind Me, Satan!* Satan? Yes, for it was the same temptation that Jesus had conquered in the wilderness, the easy way to announce His presence (Matt. 4:8). Just compromise with humanity. Do what the politicians do: Check the polls and find out what the majority want, then obey their wishes. Here was Peter; the natural leader of the apostles, repeating the very proposal of Satan at the time Christ's mission began. Jesus was no masochist who enjoyed suffering. He didn't want to die, as He pleaded to the Father in Gethsemane (Matt. 26:39). It often happens that the evil one can speak to us through the voice of one whom we love and admire. I recall somebody very dear to my heart who startled and upset me by weeping when I visited her to tell her of my decision to enter the seminary and become a priest.

His words to Peter were nearly the same as those He used to reject Satan, with a small but significant exception: *Get away from me, Satan!* was what He told the devil (Matt. 4:10). Leave Me, He implored, knowing that the evil one will do no such thing. He will return, choosing his time and situation. And if he has no respect for the Son of God, what can we expect from the devil in our own lives? Note, He tells Peter: *Get behind Me!* It's not for you to teach the Teacher, and to give advice to the Master! You have much to learn before you dare take leadership in My company. In time Peter would become leader of the Church, but not yet. He had much to learn and more to suffer, since the best and most lasting lessons remain with those who feel in their bodies and minds the instruction that lasts a lifetime.

Thirty-Third Day
HOW TO SAVE ONE'S LIFE
Mark 8:34-38

When He had called the people to himself, with his disciples also, he said to them, 'Whoever desires to come after Me, let him deny himself, and take up his cross, and follow Me. For whoever desires to save his life will lose it, but whoever loses his life for My sake and the gospel's will save it. For what will it profit a man if he gains the whole world, and loses his own soul? Or what will a man give in exchange for his soul? For whoever is ashamed of Me and My words in this adulterous and sinful generation, of him the Son of Man also will be ashamed when He comes in the glory of His Father with the holy angels.'

If only each one of us, and all of us together, would assimilate this passage in our hearts and live by its glorious message, what people we would be! What a Church God would have! What a witness we would make to the secular culture that surrounds us! Notice two points that Jesus is making: First, that He is quite plain and honest. He makes no guarantee of some method of escaping the pains and sufferings of life. The promises we frequently hear spouted from televangelists and others, luring the gullible with offers of wealth and the easy life only if they "give themselves to the Lord" is contradicted by the above announcement. Jesus sets forth a challenge, not a temptation to a life of ease and comfort.

The second aspect is that He is not telling His followers to do something that He Himself tried to avoid. *Let him deny himself and take up his cross.* Christ's entire life was one of self-denial. Once He overcame the three temptations in the wilderness: miracle, mystery and authority, He accepted loneliness, alienation, misunderstanding, suffering, rejection, punishment and crucifixion. His followers should expect similar treatment from a world that has other agendas. Quiet Andrew, the first-called apostle, never forgot this sermon. When decades later he was evangelizing among the northern tribes, he angered the local ruler for turning his subjects to Christ. "If you continue," he ranted, "I'll crucify you on the same cross you preach!" St. Andrew's reply: "If I feared the cross I would not proclaim it."

The apostle beloved by the Lord, John, was an example of the meaning of the words: *Whoever loses his life for My sake and the gospel's will save it.* Recall that on the day of Christ's crucifixion John alone had the courage to be there and watch in horror the agony of the Master's last hours of life on earth. All the others ran and hid in panic and fear — who can blame them? They were marked men. Yet John was also. The Lord's enemies were out to eradicate the entire band of Christ's "little flock." Their very speech patterns and accent would give them away. It took supreme courage and reckless, maybe even crazy love, to stand at the foot of Christ's cross. And ironically John alone of them all lived out his lifetime, escaping martyrdom.

Thirty-Fourth Day
THE TRANSFIGURATION
Mark 9:2-8

Now after six days Jesus took Peter, James, and John, and led them up on a high mountain apart by themselves; and He was transfigured before them. His clothes became shining, exceedingly white, like snow, such as no launderer on earth can whiten them. And Elijah appeared to them with Moses, and they were talking with Jesus. Then Peter answered and said to Jesus, 'Rabbi, it is good for us to be here; and let us make three tabernacles: one for You, one for Moses, and one for Elijah' — because he did not know what to say, for they were greatly afraid. And a cloud came and overshadowed them; and a voice came out of the cloud, saying, 'This is My beloved Son. Hear Him.' Suddenly, when they had looked around, they saw no one any more, but only Jesus with themselves.

It was a week after the momentous event in Caesarea Philippi, when Jesus had revealed that He indeed was the long-promised Messiah. He had described the implications of His role and prepared the disciples for what would take place. Now He took three of them off to a high mountain. He wanted them to witness to what would happen there, and to draw strength from the experience. Jesus also sought some reaffirmation of the route He was destined to take, leading eventually to His crucifixion in Jerusalem.

His listeners had always been fascinated by the way that He *spoke with His own authority*. All rabbis and scribes based their lessons on the Law and prophets. Here Jesus is seen between the writer of the Law, Moses, and the first of prophets, Elijah. The two Old Testament saints both had experiences on Mt. Sinai where the glory of the Lord had been revealed to them. They endorsed His path and confirmed what He was about to accomplish. John the Baptist heard the voice of the Father when he had baptized Jesus in the Jordan, with the very same affirmation and command.

But it was mostly on behalf of the disciples that He created for them the mountaintop experience. Surely they had been crushed by the news of what would happen to their beloved Master. Even though He explained gently in three stages the traumas which they would all endure, adding more negative incidents with each telling, nevertheless the horror of it paralyzed them with fear and challenged all sense and meaning. They were the first three, who, with Andrew, had been following Him from the beginning of His ministry. What He was relating confused their minds and broke their hearts. The meaning of this, for us, is that we often wish for something to hold onto, a sign from the Lord that He is really there; but even with faith, the world and our human reasoning cannot grasp the ways of God.

The transfiguration was a gift of glory. *Orthodox* means *right glory*. Orthodox Christians are glory people. Here were the top quarter of the apostles given a moment of glory to treasure in their hearts and comfort them through the worst of times, a gift to share with those they felt worthy of appreciating the event. Mark takes pains to try describing the brilliance of Christ in His garments, so bright that they could not look directly at Him. Moses had a similar experience on Mt. Sinai, and Elijah saw only a fleeting glimpse as the Lord had passed by. That brilliant light has not disappeared from Christ's Church. Hardly more than 150 years ago, a friend and biographer of St. Seraphim of Sarov described a similar brightness when looking at the beloved Russian saint. He said it was like trying to gaze directly at the sun.

Thirty-Fifth Day
ELIJAH'S RETURN
Mark 9:9-13

Now as they came down from the mountain, He commanded them that they should tell no one the things they had seen, till the Son of Man had risen from the dead. So they kept this word to themselves, questioning what the rising from the dead meant. And they asked Him, saying, 'Why do the scribes say that Elijah must come first?' Then He answered and told them, 'Indeed, Elijah is coming first and restores all things. And how is it written concerning the Son of man, that he must suffer many things and be treated with contempt? But I say to you that Elijah has also come, and they did to him whatever they wished, as it is written of him.'

Can you imagine what was going through the minds of the three apostles coming down from the mountain? They couldn't wait to tell the nine others of what they had experienced. Better, they might inform the Lord's persecutors, the Pharisees and scribes who said He was not a true Jew — Moses and Elijah had endorsed His credentials. But Jesus **commanded** them to say nothing until after He had risen from the grave. Not by a miracle was He to be revealed to them. If their hearts were so hardened that His healings and teachings were distorted to the degree that they said His authority came from the devil, they weren't worthy to know the truth, and they wouldn't be convinced by the report of the three apostles. They themselves didn't know what to make of it. Nothing less than the Cross and Resurrection could explain the meaning of Christ's gospel. The new element: Resurrection — what did that mean? It's clear they never quite grasped its significance. They were raised as strict Hebrews, taught to love and study the Holy Bible; but nothing there prepared them for the message of Jesus.

They added another element. The prophet Malachi predicted that before Messiah is to appear, Elijah would come to announce the event. What happened to Elijah? They knew that Jesus was the Messiah — where then is His forerunner? Jesus answered them, saying that Elijah had come in the person of John the Baptist; however, his message was not heeded. Indeed, they all knew the story of John's beheading at the hands of Herod, plotted by Herodias and inspired by the dancing of her daughter, Salome. Did they think that Elijah would be greeted with a rousing welcome and treated like a celebrity? Those who have *eyes to see and ears to hear* ought to be able to comprehend what's taking place. Is it so difficult to imagine how the Messiah would be treated by such a generation of sinners? Of course they missed His point. They wanted to believe in their own scenario for the outcome of Christ's public appearance. He was trying to pour new wine into the old wineskins of their minds, but it seemed hopeless. The old ways of thinking were too ingrained in them. Only afterwards, when He had risen and the Holy Spirit came upon them would they fathom the great mystery of God's wisdom.

And what of us, who are long since on the far side of Pentecost. What do we understand of God's glorious plan for the world?

Thirty-Sixth Day

HOW LONG SHALL HE BE WITH US?
Mark 9:14-29

And when He came to the disciples, He saw a great multitude around them, and scribes disputing with them. Immediately, when they saw Him, all the people were greatly amazed, and running to Him, greeted Him. And He asked the scribes, 'What are you discussing with them?' Then one of the crowd answered and said, 'Teacher, I brought You my son, who has a mute spirit, and whenever it seizes him, it throws him down; he foams at the mouth, gnashes his teeth, and becomes rigid. So I spoke to your disciples, that they should cast it out, but they could not.' He answered him and said, 'O faithless generation, how long shall I be with you? How long shall I bear with you? Bring him to Me.' Then they brought him to Him, and when he saw Him, immediately the spirit convulsed him, and he fell on the ground and wallowed, foaming at the mouth. So He asked his father, 'How long has this been happening to him?' And he said, 'From childhood. And often he has thrown him both into the fire and into the water to destroy him. But if You can do anything, have compassion on us and help us.' Jesus said to him, 'If you can believe, all things are possible to him who believes.' Immediately the father of the child cried out and said with tears, 'Lord, I believe; help my unbelief.' When Jesus saw the people come running together, He rebuked the unclean spirit, saying to it, 'Deaf and dumb spirit, I command you, come out of him and enter him no more!' Then the spirit cried out, convulsed him greatly, and came out of him. And he became as one dead, so that many said, 'He is dead.' But Jesus took him by the hand and lifted him up and he arose. And when He had come into the house, His disciples asked Him privately, 'Why could we not cast it out?' So He said to them, 'This kind can come out by nothing but prayer and fasting.'

Meanwhile, back at the ranch, as the cowboy movies used to say, everything is hectic and confused. Jesus walks into turmoil of confusion. A crowd is arguing with the scribes who had come to bring Jesus down and expose Him as a false teacher. They had seized the opportunity to mock the Master and ridicule His disciples. The people were happy to see Him at long last, and they ran up to greet Him. The apostles who had stayed behind were helpless to bring order to the crowd, much less to heal the epileptic son of the man who came to Jesus for a cure. Some might observe that this is much more like the Church they are familiar with, where frustration and helplessness are more prevalent than evidence of Christ's presence. It does give hope to us all.

Jesus had heavy thoughts to consider. He knew that soon He would be crucified. How could He best utilize the precious time until then? What would be of most benefit to the Father's plan, and for the well-being of God's people? Yet He didn't let those weighty problems absorb His thoughts. He took responsibility for the immediate problem. He would satisfy the man despite his weak faith. He would cast out the demon that afflicted the epileptic lad.

All too familiar is the type of person here portrayed by the father. Many master the method of projecting onto others responsibility for their own interests. He's saying in effect that he had hoped Jesus was a true miracle maker, but now he doubts His powers. It's a veiled criticism, and Jesus is aware of it: *If you believe, all things are possible* in effect tells the man that it doesn't depend on Him, but on the man's own belief. And the man claims to believe, yet asks for help in believing. He's made a significant change; from a skeptic, judging Jesus and His disciples, he recognizes that he needs more faith than he possesses. An odd request — how does one give faith to somebody without much faith of his own? But Jesus is able to work a miracle even with such paltry hope and faith. Later, the disciples asked Him privately why they had failed. They weren't the only ones lacking sufficient faith to overcome the cynicism rampant that day. It is so difficult to overcome negative thinking and lack of confidence and trust. Those capable of doing so are required to prepare themselves with a great deal of prayer and fasting.

Thirty-Seventh Day
THE END IS DRAWING NEAR
Mark 9:30-32

Then they departed from there and passed through Galilee, and He did not want anyone to know it. For He taught His disciples and said to them, 'The Son of Man is being betrayed into the hands of men, and they will kill Him. And after He is killed, He will rise on the third day.' But they did not understand this saying, and were afraid to ask Him.

Galilee was the region where He had the greatest success in proclaiming the gospel. Later, Thomas will wonder why they were to leave at all, knowing as they all did that Jerusalem would be where all His dire predictions would take place. It's not a time to be surrounded by crowds of people distracting Him from what would be the focus of His attention. Somehow He had to utilize the time allotted Him in order to impress on the hearts of His disciples and apostles the essence of His message. They didn't comprehend it all — there was so much that didn't make sense to them. Still, He had implicit faith that later on after His resurrection they would reflect on what He taught them. They would remember all His teachings and put it into a semblance of comprehension.

He had told them previously that He, *the Son of Man must suffer many things, and be rejected by the elders and chief priests and scribes, and be killed, and after three days rise again* (Mark 8:31). They had mulled over that puzzling revelation. Now He added another element: *The Son of Man is being betrayed into the hands of men*. He knows who it will be. Judas Iscariot is permitted to continue among the exalted band of twelve, Christ all the while realizing it would be he who would turn Him over to His enemies.

Oh, what a feeling, to know that you are being watched and despised. Regardless of what one does or says, even struggling to make the betrayer a special friend, it's all for nothing. Judas was not demoted. He continued to serve as treasurer of the company, the others knowing full well of his greed, and that he was skimming from the common treasury. Even at the significant Last Supper Jesus had him take a place near Him, and as a gesture of love, scooped a choice morsel of some bread and offered it to Judas. It was all to no avail: His mind was made up. From decision to deed was a matter of time.

There comes a moment when one stops deliberating over committing a sin. Up to that second it's possible to change one's mind; but after that the deed is all but accomplished. So it was that night of the Last Supper when Jesus told Judas: *What you are about to do, do quickly* (John 13:27). Spare yourself any further agony. You've made your choice.

But all that was yet to be. Here Jesus leaves the north country and wends His way southward. The others wanted to ask Him the meaning of His comments about betrayal, but they were too afraid to ask. Even bold Peter had little to say.

Thirty-Eighth Day
THE TRUE DISCIPLE'S QUALITIES
Mark 9:33-37

Then He came to Capernaum. And when He was in the house He asked them, 'What was it you disputed among yourselves on the road?' But they kept silent, for on the road they had disputed among themselves who would be the greatest. And He sat down, called the twelve, and said to them, 'If anyone desires to be first, he shall be last of all and servant of all.' Then He took a little child and set him in the midst of them. And when He had taken him in His arms, He said to them, 'Whoever receives one of these little children in my name receives Me, and whoever receives Me, receives not Me but Him who sent Me.'

Here we have a tragic misunderstanding. Jesus is meditating on what will become of Him in Jerusalem, knowing full well the way He will be rejected by all the religious groups of His nation, betrayed, captured, judged, condemned, beaten, and then crucified. His problem is to prepare the apostles for that, and more important, to prepare them to promulgate everything they had seen Him do and heard Him say. They, on the other hand, spend their time arguing with one another as to which will be leader. It's human nature to get ahead in life; but it's spiritual nature to make a way for others. Dissatisfaction is both good and bad. The positive side stimulates us to study, labor, and discover ways to improve our lives and those whom we care for. The negative side can male us insensitive to the needs of others as we clamor for attention and assert ourselves without considering the feelings of those we may harm on our climb to the top. The apostles knew they were wrong to squabble over primacy, and they were ashamed. They remained silent before the

Lord. He took it quite seriously — enough so that He called them in the house and dealt with the issue. Ambition is an ugly trait, especially when it appears within the Church. Eagerness is quite different. Jesus is turning their aspirations away from themselves and towards those whom He entrusted to their care. Be first in service. Take the lead in finding ways to help the helpless, feed the hungry, bring hope to the depressed, shower affection on those who feel rejected and unloved. You want recognition? Then surpass all the others in proclaiming the gospel in all places to everyone who has never heard of Me.

St. Paul was not present in the house in Capernaum, yet he grasped the essential teaching on humility and service. He begins his epistles introducing himself as the slave of Christ Jesus. He wore the term as a mark of honor.

A famous contemporary politician is known for his love of popularity and adulation. He left office very reluctantly, because he so enjoyed the attention. One announcer said of him "He wants to be the bride at every wedding and the corpse at every funeral." This is not the way Christ expects His leaders to behave. He demands of them humility and service to others, compassion on the poor and needy, comfort to the mourners. I recall my first years as priest at our cathedral in New York City. Serving the early liturgy, the primate of the Church, Metropolitan Leonty, would don vestments just at the consecration of the Holy Gifts, receive communion, and then hold the Cross for veneration in his right hand. His left hand held onto the episcopal staff with its ornamental cloth covering that hid his fingers. In them he enclosed money, which he would give to the elderly or crippled who came to greet him.

Thirty-Ninth Day
REWARDS AND PUNISHMENTS
Mark 9:40-43

For he who is not against us is on our side. For whoever gives you a cup of water to drink in My name, because you belong to Christ, assuredly I say to you, he will by no means lose his reward. But whoever causes one of these little ones who believe in Me to stumble, it would be better for him if a millstone were hung around his neck and he were thrown into the sea.'

For those of us born in America, it is hard to imagine what it is like to live on the border of a desert, where a cold drink of water is more than a refreshment; it's an act of gracious hospitality. The thirst bites in the mouth and the throat burns with heat. Jesus is saying that when somebody gives you a drink of water because you are a Christian, he or she is blessing the Lord, and that person will ultimately be rewarded, because He never forgets an act of kindness done to Him. Remember the parable of the sheep and goats in Matthew, where He makes the same point: *The righteous will answer Him, saying "Lord, when did we see You hungry and feed You, or thirsty and give You drink?" . . . And the King will answer and say to them, "Assuredly, I say to you, inasmuch as you did it to one of the least of these My brethren, you did it to Me"* (Matt. 25:37).

Nothing is trivial or insignificant in the eyes of the Lord. He who can tell us how many hairs are on our head notices everything. And when the time comes to tally it all up, nobody who has done a good for another will be shortchanged. But look at the rest of it. *Whoever causes one of these little ones who believes in Me to stumble* . . . A spiritual song tells of "Gentle Jesus, meek and mild." That's how everyone thinks of Him, and they are not wrong. Yet notice the stringent warning to anybody who injures a little one. He uses the verb *to stumble,* because He is leading the innocent and pure through this world and into the Kingdom of God. Woe to the one who trips a child of Christ and prevents his or her progress. What will he do to the pederasts, the child abusers, those who act out their own fantasies by using the helpless, weak, blameless, defenseless children, destroying their precious innocence forever?

But He's addressing His valued apostles and disciples as well. He had just admonished them for arguing with one another over privilege and the honor of first place among them. He wants them to know that they should have the gentleness, shyness, and eagerness to please others as most little children do. They are open to learning, they have no guile, and they answer and ask questions freely without any thought as to how they appear in others' eyes. They have a simple trust in Him, in His gospel, and in those who are blessed with the grace to lead them to the Kingdom in His name.

Those who in any way block the path of His little ones of all ages, to the Father's Kingdom, should be warned. Better for them to drown themselves than to face the punishment that awaits them on the far side of death's doors. He elaborates in the next chapter:

"Let the little children come to Me, and do not forbid them, for of such is the kingdom of God. Assuredly I say to you, whoever does not receive the kingdom of God as a little child will by no means enter it." And he took them up in His arms, laid His hands on them, and blessed them. (Mark 10:14-16)

Fortieth Day
WHEN WILL HE RETURN?
Mark 13:28-37

Now learn this parable from the fig tree. When its branch has already become tender, and puts forth leaves, you know that summer is near. So you also, when you see these things happening, know that it is near — at the doors! Assuredly I say to you, this generation will by no means pass away till all these things take place. Heaven and earth will pass away, but My words will by no means pass away. But of that day and hour no one knows, not even the angels in heaven, nor the Son, but only the Father. Take heed, watch and pray, for you do not now when the hour is. It is like a man going to a far country, who left his house and gave authority to his servants, and to each his work, and commanded the doorkeeper to watch. Watch therefore, for you do not know when the master of the house is coming — in the evening, at midnight, at the crowing of the rooster, or in the morning — lest, coming suddenly, he finds you sleeping. And what I say to you, I say to all: Watch!'

Mark is the oldest of the four gospels. It was written before the year 70, when the Temple, with all Jerusalem, was destroyed. Jesus is not predicting His Second Coming, but the fall of the Holy City. In regard to His return to the earth, He says quite honestly that He Himself doesn't know when that will happen. Only the heavenly Father knows. He left that decision to the mind of the Almighty.

The point of this passage is that watchfulness is most important, not calculations. Those whose Christianity is based on predictions of the Second Coming risk the danger of minimizing the world we now live in. One might recall the controversy over the Secretary of the Interior, James Watt, in the Reagan administration who was criticized for stating that one need not worry too much over the environment, since with Christ's reappearance, everything will be gone anyhow.

Why is it then that those who read the scriptures often fail to grasp the message therein? How is it that we have had through the ages so many who did what Jesus Himself never dared? The evangelists on the television often warn that we are living in the last days: How do they know? Of course there are signs in the Bible, in such books as Daniel, some minor prophets, and most of all in the book of Revelations. But if we trust Jesus, we shall understand that He is making a basic appeal to us. Rather than to try forecasting His return, we would be better off living in such a way that it really will not matter when He returns, because we will be prepared to receive Him. Just as the loyal, diligent, trustworthy, and industrious servants of the absent master of the house served him and performed their duties as if he had been at home all the while, so too those who love and serve the Lord feel His presence surrounding them at all times. They need not wonder about His return, because He lives in their hearts and is always with them. Their lives are spent not in pleasures of the flesh, amusements, and entertainments, or activities that they are not proud of. They are aware that their lives are limited; they have precious little time to change what needs to be altered in their attitudes and prejudices, which they simply cannot take along with them as part of their personalities when they are called to an appearance in the kingdom of the Lord.